STUDIES IN SOCIOLOGY

This series, prepared under the auspices of the British Sociological Association, is designed to provide short but comprehensive and scholarly treatments of key problem-areas in sociology. The books do not offer summary accounts of the current state of research in various fields, but seek rather to analyse matters which are the subject of controversy or debate. The series is designed to cover a broad range of topics, falling into three categories: (1) abstract problems of social theory and social philosophy; (2) interpretative questions posed by the writings of leading social theorists; (3) issues in empirical sociology. In addition, the series will carry translations of important writings in sociology which have not previously been available in English. Each book makes a substantive contribution to its particular topic, while at the same time giving the reader an indication of the main problems at issue; each carries an annotated bibliography, comprising a critical survey of relevant further literature.

ANTHONY GIDDENS

University of Cambridge

D1447680

STUDIES IN SOCIOLOGY

General Editor: ANTHONY GIDDENS

Editorial Advisers: T. B. BOTTOMORE, DAVID LOCKWOOD and ERNEST GELLNER

Published

THE SOCIOLOGY OF SOCIAL MOVEMENTS
J. A. Banks

KNOWLEDGE AND IDEOLOGY IN THE SOCIOLOGY OF EDUCATION
Gerald Bernbaum

MARXIST SOCIOLOGY
Tom Bottomore

POLITICS AND SOCIOLOGY IN THE THOUGHT OF MAX WEBER
Anthony Giddens

THE USE OF OFFICIAL STATISTICS IN SOCIOLOGY
Barry Hindess

STRIKES AND INDUSTRIAL CONFLICT: BRITAIN AND SCANDINAVIA
Geoffrey K. Ingham

PROFESSIONS AND POWER
Terence J. Johnson

POWER: A RADICAL VIEW
Steven Lukes

THE ORGANISATION OF CRIME
Mary McIntosh

CONSCIOUSNESS AND ACTION AMONG THE WESTERN WORKING CLASS
Michael Mann

THE SOCIAL PROCESS OF INNOVATION: A STUDY IN THE SOCIOLOGY OF SCIENCE
M. J. Mulkay

Forthcoming

THE DEVELOPMENT OF THE SOCIOLOGY OF KNOWLEDGE
Steven Lukes

CLASS THEORY AND THE DIVISION OF LABOUR
Gavin Mackenzie

Knowledge and Ideology in the Sociology of Education

GERALD BERNBAUM

Professor in the School of Education
University of Leicester

First edition 1977
Reprinted 1979

Published by
THE MACMILLAN PRESS LTD
London and Basingstoke
Associated companies in Delhi Dublin
Hong Kong Johannesburg Lagos Melbourne
New York Singapore and Tokyo

ISBN 0 333 15762 1

Printed in Hong Kong

CONTENTS

PREFACE

THIS short study is about the sociology of education. In particular, I have tried to set the recent developments within the subject in the context of other changes, changes in sociological theory, educational practice and educational ideologies. Though, at times, I am critical of some of the new ideas which are now available, there is a very real sense in which the present study could not have been written without the insights and perspectives which are represented by the 'new directions in the sociology of education.'

I am therefore grateful to all who have been involved in the attempt to change the sociology of education. Also (though I must not assume that they do not wish to change the sociology of education), I am grateful to Tom Whiteside and Sara Delamont for reading and commenting upon a draft of this study, and to Tony Giddens for his very helpful advice. Needless to say I accept full responsibility for the arguments developed, and the faults, particularly, remain obstinately my own.

G.B.

1. INTRODUCTION: THE 'NEW' AND 'OLD' SOCIOLOGY OF EDUCATION

IN preparing this study I have kept firmly in mind the editorial injunction that these 'books do not offer summary accounts of the current state of research . . . but seek rather to analyse matters which are the subject of controversy or debate'. Consequently, I have taken as the main theme of the book the contemporary debate about the nature of the sociology of education, and particularly that new direction which urges that the sociology of education should move towards the sociology of knowledge.

There is a sense, therefore, in which the exercise is, itself, one in the sociology of knowledge with its centre of interest as the sociology of education. It is true, of course, that the new directions in the sociology of education are inseparable from other developments in sociological theory. It will be an important part of the arguments to be developed here that the prescribed changes within the sociology of education must be seen in the wider context of changes elsewhere in sociology – a context which will serve to illuminate their own origins and thus serve to explain them more coherently. I have adopted this approach because the impact of these new perspectives upon the work of the Open University, colleges and departments of education has already been significant, yet the more recent arguments have not themselves been subjected to any over-all critical appraisal. Furthermore, the discussion by the advocates of the 'new' sociology of education of what has passed for the conventional sociology of education does, in my view, require serious modification in the light of the partial and somewhat confused fashion in which they have chosen to handle it.

I am concerned, therefore, with the 'production' of the sociology of education and the ways its concerns come to be limited, defined and evaluated. Thus the relationships between sociology and educational ideologies and practice will be explored in order

A*

to demonstrate the penetration of much sociological thought in the field of education by ideologies of a political and educational kind. Moreover, this interpenetration will be shown to be an important factor in both the 'new' and 'old' sociology of education. In no sense, however, do I wish to develop arguments which serve to undermine the bases of all knowledge or of knowledge within the sociology of education. Quite the reverse, for my main purpose involves assessing the implications and consequences of the ways in which the sociology of education is related to an 'educational' context which influences, and largely determines, the choice of research problems, availability and diffusion of findings, and the normative climate in which sociological evidence is used to consider 'solutions' to educational problems. I am anxious, therefore, to examine the sociology of education, both new and old, within a framework which encompasses, on the one hand, changes in sociological theory, and, on the other, changes in educational policies, practice and ideologies.

It will be helpful to begin the discussion with a clear understanding of the recent developments in the sociology of education which have largely been associated with the publication of *Knowledge and Control*, and linked to the ideas of that book's editor, Michael F. D. Young. It will be difficult to avoid lengthy discussion of Young's work, and though, in certain respects, I will be critical of the arguments he has employed, it will remain true that his novel approach to the sociology of education has stimulated an interest in the subject and a debate within it whose benefits in enlivening the area of enquiry are still to be fully recognised. Moreover, there is a provocativeness about Young's work which has been missing from much writing in the sociology of education during the late 1960s, and a very real sense in which the present contribution could not have been made without benefit of the perspectives he has developed. It will be important to note, however, that Young's own views have changed over time and a full examination will make it necessary to incorporate his newest ideas along with those which date from the appearance of *Knowledge and Control*.

In *Knowledge and Control* Young has drawn especial attention to some of the deficiencies of the conventional sociology of education, particularly those parts of it concerned with the class

10

determinants of educability. Following Seeley, Young argues that, 'on the whole, sociologists have "taken" educators' problems, and, by not making them explicit, have necessarily taken them for granted'.[1] Moreover, Young points out that these implicit assumptions of educators and sociologists are characterised by an 'order' doctrine which leads to explanations in terms of a systems perspective. Developing this standpoint, Young can, therefore, criticise much of the early work on social class and educational opportunity, which has for so long dominated the sociology of education. He argues that work of this kind treats as unproblematic 'what it is to be educated', and therefore provides little more than a dubious legitimacy for the various pressures for piecemeal administrative and curricular reform.

Young's alternative view of the sociology of education is that it should lead to questions being asked about how pupils, teachers and knowledge are organised. It is central to this initial stage of Young's arguments that sociologists shall not treat the dominant legitimising categories of educationalists as absolute, but should view them as constructed realities which are realised in particular institutional contexts. In this fashion sociologists will come to treat educators' problems as phenomena to be explained. As Young urges, 'existing categories that for parents, teachers, children and many researchers distinguish home from school, learning from play, academic from non-academic, and "able" or "bright" from "dull" or "stupid", must be conceived of as socially constructed, with some in a position to impose their constructions or meanings on others'.[2] Even more forcefully, Young asserts that the 'dogmas of rationality and science become open to enquiry: the necessary preliminary to conceiving of alternatives'.[3]

It follows from these arguments that what Young is advocating is that the sociology of education should ask questions about the social organisation of knowledge in educational institutions, and that consequently 'the sociology of education is no longer conceived as the area of enquiry distinct from the sociology of knowledge'.[4] Young also hints at the ways in which the new approaches he is advocating might alter the nature of research structuring in the subject. Following Gouldner, he suggests that interactional studies must be supported by efforts to conceptualise the associa-

11

tions between interaction and changing social structures. According to Young it will follow that what will then be treated as problematic in the sociology of education is the set of social conventions which are generally accepted for the prescribers (say, the teachers), and in this way the direction of research will be towards a sociology of educational knowledge which will 'explore how and why certain dominant categories persist and the nature of their possible links to sets of interests and activities such as occupational groupings'.[5]

Moreover, Young is clear about the research implications of his own position. He argues that 'the sociology of education . . . must take into account the historical and situationally specific character of both its phenomena and its explanations',[6] and that 'very detailed case studies are necessary which treat as problematic the curricula, pedagogic and assessment categories held by school personnel'. Again, therefore, Young is in a position to argue that research in the classroom and the school can ask questions about everyday distinctions such as right and wrong, strict and slack, interesting and dull, which themselves become phenomena to be explained.

Clearly, these new perspectives draw heavily upon changes occurring elsewhere in the social sciences. Thus Young's ideas owe a great deal to Kuhn's work on changes in science and to his central argument that 'as science progresses its concepts are repeatedly destroyed and replaced'.[7] Young draws upon recent work in anthropology, especially that of Horton,[8] to suggest that there is a parallel between the reluctance of the conventional anthropologist to take his respondent's ideas at their face value as the explanations they claim to be, and the reluctance of sociologists to treat as problematic the hierarchical definitions of ability that are held by most teachers and pupils – definitions which then become institutionalised in conventional educational arrangements. Similarly, Young's work and that of his associates have close links with the renewed interests in phenomenological approaches within the social sciences. It is not surprising, therefore, to find Young quoting Douglas[9] with approval, and arguing that sociology should be concerned with the subversion of absolutism. Such a view Young believes to be of crucial importance for the sociology of education, as it would enable challenges to be made to many of the existing hierarchical categories and even to definitions of 'the teachers' and 'the taught'.

I have deliberately given time to setting out Young's arguments as they have been presented in *Knowledge and Control*. They seem to me to represent most sensitively and coherently the case against the conventional sociology of education and also to point to an alternative which has, to some extent, been realised in research. The 'new directions' have, moreover, been widely diffused through the education courses of the Open University. These courses are mainly for teachers and, as Eggleston[10] has noted, may have contributed to the uncertainty which now surrounds a great deal of the research and data in the sociology of education. The impact of Young's work has been, therefore, very significant. It is even possible to argue that there are now two sociologies of education. As Williamson has proposed, the current development of the new perspective has affected 'the assumptions in terms of which this activity of thinking sociologically about education has been embraced. There is hardly a lecture course in the land unaffected by it.'[11]

Williamson goes on to argue that the new sociology of education provides us with an intriguing example of curriculum change which cries out to be analysed in its own right, and it is the basis of the present study that Young's own general position contains interesting possibilites for beginning the study of the development of the sociology of education. An approach, therefore, which enquires into the origins and nature of the sociology of education will enable questions to be asked about the ways in which, and the degrees to which, sociologists concerned with education have accepted the dominant categories of educationalists and teachers. It will encourage an investigation of the extent to which the whole area of enquiry has been dominated by the structural-functionalist perspectives of the parent discipline and of the consequences of any such domination. It will help us to establish the conditions and processes by which teaching and research relevant to the curricula of the sociology of education have been selected and institutionalised in educational organisations, and to explore any relationships between these developments and the careers of the personnel engaged in teaching and research. It should be possible, therefore, to give some substance to the desire to account for the

13

historical and situationally specific character of the explanations offered in the sociology of education, both those of the dominant school, and also of those derived from the more recent and radical reconsiderations of theory and method in the social sciences. Quite simply, as Popper has pointed out, those who advocate the perspectives of the sociology of knowledge 'invite the application of their own methods to themselves with an almost irresistible hospitality'.[12]

An approach such as I am recommending will have the merit of ridding much of the current debate within the subject of its arid and ahistorical quality. Moreover, it will facilitate an elaboration of a neglected area of Young's own arguments. One of Young's major criticisms of the sociology of education as it has been conventionally practised is that it has too readily rested upon a dominant structural-functionalist framework. Critics of this framework argue that it has encouraged sociologists to believe that their work is value-free and that it deals in objective data. As far as education is concerned this approach, it is argued, has led sociologists to analyse 'problems' of the system largely as these have come to be defined by teachers and administrators. In this way Young points out that the sociology of education has had amongst its primary features questions relating to the the promotion of equality of educational opportunity, to the efficient running of schools and to the control of educational deviants. According to Young one of the major deficiencies of this perspective is that it neglects the questions concerned with the principles of selection and organisation of knowledge and curricula, and with the institutional and interactional settings in schools and classrooms. In order to explain the deficiency Young argues that it is necessary to examine 'on the one hand the ideological and methodological assumptions of the sociologists, and on the other hand the institutional context within which the sociological study of education has developed'.[13] In substance, however, Young devotes very little space or time to this examination, and it is possible to argue that there are inadequacies in what he does have to say about these important areas of investigation.

Young's brief explanation of the kind of sociology of education we have had is of a conventional nature. He points out that in the late 1950s much British sociology, and in particular the sociology

14

of education, was based upon the sentiments of Fabian socialism and the methodology of the demographic tradition drawn from Booth and Rowntree. According to Young this led sociologists away from a concern with poverty to an awareness of a lack of education as an important feature of poverty, and hence to an overwhelming concern with inequality and the characteristics of working-class failures. In turn, the work of sociologists could be used to lend support to reformists social policies. Young characterises this work by its essential concern with a narrow interest in stratification rather than in education, and argues that the sociologists 'were concerned to show how the distribution of life chances through education can be seen as an aspect of the class structure.[14] He believes, moreover, that this led, inevitably, to the isolation of the 'class' characteristics of individuals from the 'class' content of their educational experience.

In dealing with the institutional context of the sociology of education, Young admits that what he has to say is only speculative but he offers a brief explanation in terms of an arbitrary division of labour in colleges, institutes and departments of education. Thus, the practitioners of the sociology of education, whose contribution to the academic study of education has only developed over the last fifteen years, found that in institutions devoted to the study of education, philosophers and school-subject specialists had already laid claim to matters relating to curriculum and pedagogy. Sociologists, therefore, pursued their own interests in such a way as to minimise boundary disputes and to concentrate upon the unexplored areas of the college teaching and the college curriculum. In this way, according to Young, there developed the concern with the social context of education, social class, relationships between education and the economy, the occupational structure and the family, schools as organisations and pupil sub-cultures.

Given the speculative nature of Young's discussion, it is not surprising that it is possible to develop alternative arguments which emphasise different explanatory elements in the development of sociological investigation in the field of education. As already noted, Young explains the inadequacies of the sociology of education by examining on the one hand the ideological and methodological assumptions of the sociologists, and on the other

15

hand the institutional context within which the sociological study of education has developed. It is possible, however, that he emphasises those features of the sociology of education which best suit the case he is trying to make. Thus, by choosing to emphasise the origins of educational studies in terms of stratification, he is in a position to strengthen his assertion about functionalist perspectives dominating the area of enquiry and to enhance his criticisms of the influence of 'order' doctrines and 'system perspectives'. Young's attack, however, on the early work in the sociology of education draws attention away from the actual development of the subject of the sociology of education and lends itself to Popper's general criticism of the sociology of knowledge – its failure to understand the social aspects of knowledge.

Similarly, it is possible to challenge the view that the form the sociology of education has taken has been seriously determined by the prior presence of philosophers in colleges of education. There is little evidence to suggest that they had laid claim to matters relating to curriculum and pedagogy, and consequently they are unlikely to have prevented sociologists from moving into areas allied to the sociology of knowledge. Indeed, Peters, who has been so concerned with the transformation of philosophy within the field of education has distinguished two types of philosophy which were institutionalised in colleges in the mid-1960s. First, there is that concerned with principles of education, which he describes as being concerned with the cementation of values, the dispensing of wisdom about education. As Peters has written, this 'task is partly a relic of the old conception of the philosopher as a kind of oracle'.[15] Second, Peters points out how the dispensation of wisdom is often reinforced with 'supports from what the great educators of the past have said about it . . . a Cook's tour of thinkers from Plato to Dewey'.[16] If Peters's analysis has any merit, then it casts doubt on Young's view which attributes at least some of the features of the sociology of education to the philosophers' concern with curriculum and pedagogy.

It is being suggested here, therefore, that one of the major weaknesses of Young's discussion is that he fails to apply his general argument concerning the nature of the social organisation of knowledge in educational institutions to the sociology of education itself. Most especially, despite exhortations concerning

16

desirable changes to be made in the sociology of education, Young does not exhibit sufficient concern for the 'historical and situationally specific' features of the subject with which he is concerned. It will be helpful, therefore, to examine the development of the sociology of education in terms of the discussion of particular research problems and also in the context of the organisation of teaching and curricula in colleges and departments of education.

Central to any such discussion must be the review article of Floud and Halsey published in 1958.[17] In this article Floud and Halsey, whose early work in the sociology of education is the target of many of Young's strictures on the subject, set out their views of the development of the field and suggest criticisms of the work conducted up to that time. It is interesting to note the ways in which their points of view on development and criticism differ from those of Young, and also the degree to which, in some respects, they anticipate him. Most importantly, however, Floud and Halsey set the ideological issues relevant to the sociology of education in a different framework from that of Young, by understanding more clearly the historical development of the subject.

Floud and Halsey claim a recognisable history for the sociology of education from the appearance of Ward's *Dynamic Sociology* in 1883. In this work, Ward argued against Spencer's pessimistic view of social studies and urged that education could be an essential force in progress. From its beginning, therefore, the sociology of education might be seen to be associated with human betterment. As Floud and Halsey noted, however, this 'was to prove a doubtful blessing for the disciplined development of the field'.[18] More especially was this the case once pragmatism and educational reform became so dominant at the turn of the century. The perspectives of James, Pierce and Dewey openly injected normative elements into the study of education at a time when a great deal of the work was already suffering from methodological deficiencies. This American experience in the formation of the discipline has its equivalent elsewhere. In Germany and Britain, for example, the early development of the subject was dominated by various kinds of socialist ideology, and in the 1930s at the London School of Economics the systematic study

17

of education was undertaken with its main interest focused upon the part played by educational arrangements 'in producing and perpetuating class differences and in promoting social mobility'.[19]

Following 1945, Floud and Halsey point out that in both Britain and the United States most of the work had 'its normative orientations unimpaired',[20] and that a great deal of it, especially the choice of research problems, was strongly influenced by socialist beliefs. From the perspective of the present study, therefore, what is worthy of note is that the sociology of education as it has developed in Britain and the United States has been influenced by ideological considerations. In general terms, the approaches of the sociologists working in the field of education have been progressive and reformist, and, in an eclectic fashion, they have drawn upon socialist political ideologies and progressive educational ideologies. In part, at least, this helps to explain why so much of this work lacks any strict or coherent theoretical basis. Nevertheless, by the 1950s sociologists of education had accepted in some form the theoretical perspective of the increasingly dominant structural-functionalist school, and though Floud and Halsey are critical of the influence of this body of thought, they nevertheless advocated approaches which seem to offer some support to it.

In pointing out the deficiencies of much of the work in the sociology of education in the period up to 1958, Floud and Halsey anticipated many of the more modern criticisms of structural-functionalism and the ways in which sociologists in the field of education too readily adopted it from anthropology. Thus they argued that structural-functionalist perspectives are too easily concerned with social equilibrium and with social integration based upon consensus. As far as education is concerned, therefore, it is too readily viewed as a means of motivating individuals to behave in ways appropriate to maintain the society in a state of equilibrium. Clearly, Floud and Halsey believed that in a 'technological' society characterised by social change, notions of 'consensus' and 'integration' can only be loosely maintained. In advanced industrial societies the problems of analysis with respect to educational institutions lie in seeing them in their diverse relations with the wider social structure. If for sociological

18

purposes they are treated exclusively in terms of their supposed contribution to individual socialisation and social cohesion the effect is to over-simplify. In these highly differentiated societies consensus cannot be understood in terms of shared values nor integration determined by this kind of consensus.

The adoption of structural-functionalist perspectives has therefore weakened sociologists' ability to explain social change and this has exaggerated the penetration into the sociology of education of the normative perspectives derived from the American pragmatists and the European socialists. This has come about precisely because the dominant ethos of education has been one of improvement, and thus of change, both at an individual and a societal level. The failure of sociologists, possibly due to the orientations of structural-functionalism, to explicate change has encouraged the normative and ideological perspectives of the educationalists.

It can be seen, therefore, that as early as 1958 two of the leading British sociologists of education were able to offer a systematic and coherent critique of their subject in terms not totally dissimilar from the more modern analyses of the new sociologists of education. The two main points they make concerned the influence of structural-functionalist perspectives upon the sociology of education. Difficulties arose, they argue, from the initial anthropological influences on the sociology of education and the association of the subject with the normative judgements and political ideologies of educationalists.

With the benefit of hindsight it is interesting to note the ways in which other of Floud and Halsey's criticisms anticipated some of the more recent debates. Thus they urged that what is required is a more detailed study of educational institutions. Indeed, they emphasised the ways in which studies of educational wastage are one-sided, concentrating too much on home background and family environment without asking sufficient questions about 'the assumptions, values and aims embodied in the school organisation', and concluded that 'the historically determined aims and organisation of these institutions (schools and colleges) and the tacit changes of social function they have undergone must be understood'.[21]

This review by Floud and Halsey has, unfortunately, been

neglected by recent critics, yet there is much in it that would add variety and subtlety to their analyses. Thus, Floud and Halsey readily admitted the normative features of the sociology of education but not in such a way that attributed its appearance to sociological theory. Rather, they understood the influences of the setting of the discipline and the specific qualities of its growth in the context of the study of education. Thus they were in a position to discuss the inter-war debate in the United States concerning the nature of 'educational sociology' and whether it was a branch of education or of sociology. This debate was repeated significantly in post-war England.

Moreover, it is also interesting to consider the more positive side of the critique offered by Floud and Halsey. Despite their apparent uncertainty concerning the influence of structural-functionalism upon the sociology of education, they could not avoid a macro-sociological analysis of their own which tacitly admitted such a perspective and did so in a context which presaged the more recently developed technocratic theories of society and the place of education in such a society. According to Floud and Halsey, none of the acknowledged early masters who wrote about education – Durkheim, Weber, or Mannheim – 'seems to have faced the fundamental difficulty in the sociology of education; namely, that of prescribing an orderly and coherent analysis of a set of institutions which by their nature confound social-psychological and sociological issues, straddling as they do the psychology and the organisational structure of society.'[22] They argued, moreover, that this fundamental difficulty is exaggerated in a consideration of advanced industrial societies where there are complex, formal and specialised educational institutions which function in close relation to, but in partial independence of, the wider social structure. For Floud and Halsey, in advanced industrial societies, or 'technological' societies, new burdens are thrown upon educational institutions – the burdens of mass instruction, occupational recruitment, social selection, promotion of scientific and technological progress. Indeed, according to them,

under conditions of advanced industrialism . . . the economy becomes increasingly dominated by the institutions of research and technological innovation, with the result that the differentiation of educational institutions and functions assumes new proportions. So much is this so that the educational system comes to occupy a strategic place as a central determinant of the economic, political, social and cultural character of society.[28]

I think it is true to say that, despite their own general criticisms, Floud and Halsey adopt an essentially functionalist perspective. Moreover, it can be argued that their view was the dominant one throughout the 1960s. Their approach was well suited to the apparently consensual nature of supposedly affluent societies and the confidence evinced, by many authors, in the future of those advanced societies. As far as education is concerned, such views lent themselves to the optimistic conjunction of two different but related ideologies. It became possible for advocates of educational change and expansion to justify their case not only on the varied grounds of social justice but also on grounds of national economic efficiency. The marriage of these ideas is already implicit in the sections quoted from Floud and Halsey, and though it is not possible in a work of this kind to explore in detail the changes in political ideologies over the course of this century, it is clear that by the 1950s and 1960s social justice through the provision of equal educational opportunity was explicitly linked to the concept of economic efficiency and growth. Nor were these principles seen as being the source of potential conflict, rather they served to provide mutual justification.

Sociologists and politicians asserted that in the developing world massive educational expenditure was necessary to provide, on the one hand, the 'take-off' for economic growth, and on the other, the conditions for the survival of democratic institutions. In the advanced industrial societies, education was seen as offering the key condition of continued economic growth by providing trained and skilled manpower capable of exploiting to the full developments in applied science and technology. Thus, as Jean Floud urged, 'a modern economy depends on maximising the educational output of every individual', and 'in a modern economy the quality and efficiency of the working population

21

very largely depend on the educational system'.[24] In the same discussion Swedish contributors indicated that the issues of social justice and economic growth were conjoined in their own society. De Wolff and Härnqvist urged that

> the interest in higher education in modern society springs from two sources. One is of ethical origin and is related to the growing belief that every individual, regardless of his social status and origin, should be given equal opportunity for education up to the highest level. The other is economic and has its origin in the recognition that qualified manpower is a fundamental factor of production.[25]

Now, these concerns for social justice, equal opportunity and economic growth can be well documented in the official definitions of educational policy which have emerged since 1945. The government reports and legislation are replete with illustrations which show the nature of their concerns. The 1956 *White Paper on Technical Education* argued that other countries were making determined efforts to train more scientific and technical manpower and that Britain, too, must make a determined effort, the aims being 'to strengthen the foundations of our economy, to improve the standards of living of our people'.[26] The *Crowther Report* of 1959 was even more explicit: 'If we are to build a higher standard of living – and, what is more important, if we are to have higher standards in life – we shall need a firmer educational base than we have today. Materially and morally, we are compelled to go forward.'[27] In advocating the raising of the school-leaving age, the authors of the report adduced two main arguments: 'one starts from the social and personal needs of 15-year-olds, and regards education as one of the basic rights of the citizen; the other is concerned with education as a vital part of the nation's capital investment.'[28] Moreover, similar arguments were developed by members of the Committee on Higher Education (the *Robbins Report*) to support the expansion of the tertiary sector of education. Thus they noted in their guiding principles, 'we do not believe that modern societies can achieve their aims of economic growth and higher cultural standards without making the most of the talents of their

22

citizens. . . . The good society desires equality of opportunity for its citizens to become not merely good producers but also good men and women.[29]

It was not only the official reports, however, which emphasised the ways in which the functions of education were supposedly changing. Vaizey, for example, whose views have been very important in shaping educational policy, argued in the early 1960s that

> ours is an affluent society because our knowledge of the physical and social world is expanding at a fantastic rate . . . education helps to strengthen the economy for it is an investment in manpower. . . . Education is important, therefore, not only to help our children, to give them better lives, to improve the society in which we live, to enable this country to go forward paying its way and competing internationally; but it is essential if we are to survive in a changing, technical and scientific age.[30]

In the mid-1960s an American sociologist showed how these things might come to be realised at the school level:

> As the society changes technologically, it is apparent that the educational system must keep pace with it. Not only must the schools turn out individuals who are capable of keeping the machines on which the society depends running but even more importantly they must also provide the remainder of the population with the knowledge, skills and sophistication necessary to adapt successfully to the multitude of changes occurring around them and to solve whatever new problems are generated by current technological innovations. . . . If continued development and change are deemed desirable, schools must assume the added responsibility of preparing certain members of the society to take an active part in the change process. The primary effect of all this on the school is to make mandatory continual changes in what is taught, even at fairly basic instructional levels.[31]

Moreover, it is clear that such general beliefs about the nature of the future have recently been reflected in programmes

23

for individual schools which are increasingly based on assumptions about the future, involving a society of rapid technological change, a sizeable diminution of manual jobs and increasing leisure. Thus the senior staff of one notably innovative school have written :

> We hope to educate children for the world they will live in, the world of 1975–2025 – not the world of the last fifty years; we believe this means the all-round development of brain, personality and body. To think rather than to mèmorise; to develop high skills in all forms of communication . . . to earn a living in a world in which work, for some, becomes increasingly technological – and in itself subject to change – for others, involves greater contacts with people, and yet for others, becomes duller in content and shorter in duration.[32]

Underpinning this sample of arguments are sets of assumptions which relate closely to simple functionalist views of society and particularly to the links between education, the economy and the occupational order, and also to the growing number of technocratic theories of society which attempt to describe the future of the advanced industrial societies by extrapolating certain contemporary features of modern American society. It is interesting to remember, however, that the sociologists of education have readily adopted many stances which are essentially the same.

Even more significantly, and showing closely how it became possible to link together notions of social justice and economic efficiency, Floud and Halsey argued that :

> the notion that an advanced industrial economy requires a well educated, adaptable and fluid – i.e. geographically and occupationally mobile – labour force is implicit in our account of the growing involvement of education and economy. Ideally, runs the implication, talent should find its own level in the market, and the only guarantees that it may possibly do so lie in a high rate of social mobility and the minimising or elimination of social factors in educational selection and occupational recruitment.'[33]

What is remarkable about this sum of opinion is, first, the confidence with which they describe the present and the future nature of advanced industrial societies, and, second, the inter-penetration of sociological theory, educational research, and educational and political policy.

Beginning with the central position of science and technology in modern societies, there is a clear conviction that in such socie-ties the labour force is less concerned with direct manufacture and more concerned with the provision of diverse services. Accordingly, a new importance is given to education. At a societal level, education can be seen as the crucial investment, the con-dition for sustained economic growth. At an individual level, education can be seen as the key to social mobility.

In this context, therefore, the association of sociological re-search in education with the ideologies relating to educational policy is more readily explicated. The post-war period gave rise to both a sociological and an educational confidence. The socio-logical confidence is manifest in certain examples of structural-functionalism which have been recently criticised by Gouldner[34] and many others, and which have emphasised the 'consensual' aspects of Western societies in a period of economic growth. The educational confidence is reflected in the easy belief in the efficacy of educational policy to facilitate social change. Those working in the field of education, consequently, could adopt a relatively optimistic standpoint – education was crucial for economic growth, and the expansion of educational systems would bring about a great degree of social justice. Such social justice was seen to be not only desirable in its own right, but also important to maximise the talent available within the society. It was never assumed, of course, that this would necessarily occur without tension or occasional difficulty. But there were obvious educational measures which could be taken to facilitate the transformation. Along with the expansion of educational systems went a special concern to diminish the influence of selection and to promote common secondary schools. Equally of course the balance of sociological research suggested that the 'environment' or the 'family' might prevent all groups from realising the pro-mise held out by the affluent society.

Sociological research in education has been, therefore, to a

25

large degree concerned with the issues relating to social class, implicitly adopting the theoretical perspectives of the functionalist theory of social stratification established by Davis and Moore, and, somewhat differently, by Parsons. These writers have argued that social stratification inevitably occurs in complex societies such as those which have undergone industrialisation, but that it perfoms 'vital functions' for those societies. Simply put, the argument is that in a society in which tasks are specialised some will call for qualities which are not widely available amongst the individual members of the society, whilst others will call for qualities which are widely distributed. It is necessary, the argument runs, that the more talented be placed in those occupations which demand their skills. Thus occupations which demand special intellectual, administrative and entrepreneurial skills are vital to the whole society and must be rewarded by great prestige and material returns. It is admitted by proponents of this view of social stratification that, over time, the possession of great wealth, prestige and power may enable privileges to be passed on through the family system from one generation to the next. They argue, nevertheless, that there will also be social mobility which will allow the unsuccessful to lose their position, and others possessing special abilities to rise. It is clear that a sociology of education which adopts essentially functionalist perspectives in explaining in general terms the relationship of the educational system to the wider society and to other parts of that society is also likely to be a sociology of education which will concentrate at the specific level upon those areas which seem to inhibit the free movement of talent and the creation of talent. Thus in education the major work is on social class and educational opportunity, on family socialisation and selection.

here
strategic importance
of Bus. Schools
as sites for research.

2. AN ACCOUNT OF THE SOCIOLOGY OF EDUCATION: I

THUS far, therefore, I have concentrated upon explaining the relationship between the origins of sociological enquiry in the field of education and the diverse elements of that sociological theory that have been deemed relevant. I have shown how the interpenetrations by political and educational ideologies of sociological research in the field of education can be seen as bringing about not so much a legitimation of existing practices as a challenge to them. The emergence of the twin objectives of economic efficiency and social justice represented an implicit critique of the educational arrangements by which talent was manifestly 'wasted'. It is true, of course, that if the advocated educational reform had been fully and efficiently implemented, there would not have been a revolutionary transformation of the basis of the society such as might be urged by some contemporary authors. This, however, was not how the critics of, say the 1940s and 1950s, saw the issue. For them, given the relationship which existed between social class and educational opportunity and the dominance of the kinds of sociological theory that I have described, it seemed clear that they were engaged in pursuing policies which would lead to a richer and more socially just society in which certain major forms of privilege would be diminished. The discussion based on Floud and Halsey's paper on the origins of the sociology of education has enabled me, therefore, to explore some of the ideological elements in much of the early work. Indeed, as soon as the discussion moves into this area of consideration an immediate paradox arises. Whereas Young and his associates complain that sociologists of education have too readily accepted the definitions of teachers and administrators and their taken-for-granted definitions, other sociologists have noted the benefits brought about by the ways in which the sociology of education has challenged conventional and estab-

27

lished notions of the processes implicit in educational organisation.

Burns, for example, chose to illustrate his inaugural lecture, 'Sociological Explanation', by reference to those studies of social class and educational opportunity of which Young is dismissive. The over-all point which Burns wished to make was that it was precisely that kind of work which was so instrumental in challenging the assumptions of those who were responsible for the 1944 Education Act and its operation. He argues that there are no grounds for challenging the genuineness and sincerity of those who framed and administered the Act, and who later implemented the selective arrangements which he describes as fair. Yet, in his own words 'a series of studies carried out during the 1950's demonstrated conclusively that equality of opportunity had certainly not been achieved. . . . During the 1960's the considerations or assumptions treated as external to the frame of reference of education, or disregarded entirely, have been added to by educational sociologists.'[1] By generalising this argument, Burns concludes that 'the role of educational sociology is to examine, to question, to raise doubts about, to criticise the assumptions on which current policy, current theory and current practice are based'.[2] Now all of this does not necessarily contradict the view of the subject proposed by Young, but it does at least cast doubts on his description of the development of the sociology of education. His arguments are essentially ahistorical, and neglect the ways in which, and the circumstances in which, the sociology of education has in fact challenged the conventional assumptions of teachers, legislators and administrators.

Edward Boyle, for example, has little doubt about the influence of the work of sociologists on his own thinking when he was Minister of Education, and also upon the policy of the Department of Education and Science. Indeed he confirms the view of the contribution of sociology in terms strikingly similar to those of Burns. Boyle asserts there was

one respect in which the world of 1961–63 was different from the world of the 1950's. The work of these people [Floud and Halsey] made one realise that the pool of potential ability was deeper than we'd thought, and that the interplay between nature and nurture was more subtle than used to be accepted.

... The 11+ system, the emphasis on the G-Factor and intelligence were the egalitarianism of the 1920's and 1930's – a way of selecting the 'able poor'. It was the educational sociologists who showed that as measured in terms of people who got the benefits from the system, this could not be true.[3]

It is possible to argue that what in fact brought about the 'different world' to which Boyle refers was precisely the commitment of the early sociologists of education to generally left-wing political stances and their desires for a more just and equal society. These objectives they readily felt could be realised through the educational system. Indeed the lack of a value-free approach amongst the leading sociologists of education has already been strongly noted by Bantock.[4] He tries to show that, underlying the research of Floud and Halsey, there are a series of judgements and commitments which are not normally taken to be part of a descriptive and analytical sociology. Thus he points out that they hoped, in their own words, 'to throw light on the problems of providing equality of opportunity in post-war English education', and that they have done this in the context of what they choose to describe as 'the study of our outmoded but by no means moribund class structure'.[5] Bantock, moreover, takes up the explicitly prescriptive elements in the work of Floud and Halsey, in particular their clear recommendations in the early 1960s that English secondary education should be reorganised along comprehensive lines and their advocacy of schemes of vocational guidance.

In addition it should be noted that the educational reports of the 1950s and early 1960s, Early Leaving, Crowther and Robbins, were major sources of data for sociologists, yet they were, at the same time, frankly prescriptive. It was for these reasons that they were important factors in bringing about a change in public debate concerning education and a change in government policy. The political, ideological and committed quality of much of the early sociological work in the field of education, of which Bantock complains, was in fact an influence in the achievement of educational policies and reform – comprehensive education, de-streaming and diminution of psychological testing – which were seen as leading to a more just, democratic and efficient society. In the end it might be possible to argue that part of the consequences of this activity was to legitimise reformist policies, but to concentrate solely upon those consequences and hence to dismiss the work is to ignore the institutional, political and ideological contexts in which the research problems came to be defined. If the development and nature of the sociology of education are to be adequately explained it is necessary to look at more than the consequential political policies which might have been developed from the sociological investigation. Only in this way will it be possible to begin to understand the nature of the research problem and its definition by those at the time, and hence to consider the constant dialectic between educational practice and policy on the one hand and educational research on the other. The sociological studies in the field of education which were conducted in the 1940s and 1950s grew out of the educational and political context of that period. The political and educational debate of the inter-war years had been about resources, access and equality of opportunity. Until the sociologists began their work, much of the debate was conducted without anything that might be regarded as 'evidence', other than that provided by the mental testing of the psychologists. The sociological enquiries brought to light considerations and factors relating to educational performance, which, though now familiar to us all, had simply not been taken into account in the post-war attempts to produce changes in the educational system through political, ideological and administrative means.

It is important, in addition, that a discussion of the nature of the sociology of education pays full attention to the ideological and structural climate of the pursuit of educational studies. It is essential, for example, to elaborate the influence of the normative ethos of the study of education upon the 'production' of knowledge for the consumption of students within colleges and departments of education. Considerations of this kind will enable the consequences of the interpenetration of educational ideologies upon the nature of sociological enquiry in the field of education to be shown.

In certain respects the development of the sociology of education in Britain has had much in common with its growth in the United States, and Brim has indicated the over-all features of the

30

sociology of education in that country when he reports that

> The fact is that much of what passes under the name of socio-
> logical training of educators is carried on by persons trained in
> education not sociology. One must recognise that unfortu-
> nately the materials presented are frequently pseudosociology,
> consisting of moralistic and philosophical content rather than
> research and theory. They may be variously termed, such as
> social stratification, community organisation, or the family,
> but they often turn out to be sociology in name only.'[6]

There is little doubt, however, that these problems have occur-
red in Britain also. The nature of the debate is well illustrated
by a consideration of the contributions made to the journal
Education for Teaching, which is the publication of the professional association which represents college-of-education staff. The
articles, appearing over the last fifteen years or so, have discussed
regularly the principles involved in teaching sociology in the
colleges and given representative examples of syllabuses. Thus in
1961 Taylor, in a contribution designed to present a syllabus of
the sociology of education for the colleges, made the distinction,
echoing American experience, between 'educational sociology'
and 'sociology of education', the latter being more rigorous, and
more likely to satisfy the standards of the professional sociologists.
Taylor warned that there is 'little point in calling part of a college
of education course "sociological" when in fact the topics con-
sidered would not be recognised as being within their legitimate
province'.[7]

There is substantial evidence, however, that Taylor's warnings have not been heeded. Throughout the 1960s articles
appeared regularly which advocated the benefits of sociology in
terms of the special insights that the teacher is supposed to require for handling working-class children, or for the contribution
that it can make to the over-all 'efficiency' of the educational
system. The enquiries of MacGuire[8] at the beginning of the
1960s and Shipman[9] at the end of the decade both show the
diverse and eclectic nature of sociology in the colleges of education.
They demonstrate that the college courses tended, during a time
of rapid growth and expansion, to lack any systematic discussion

of theoretical or methodological issues, and that there was 'an absence of crucial areas such as power, conflict, socialisation and social control'.[10] Popular elements in the sociology courses were those that reflected a problem-orientated approach and which did not challenge the prevailing educational ideologies – topics such as probation, child guidance, delinquency, leisure and the mass media, and adolescence.

Moreover, it is not only sociology which has developed special characteristics as it has been incorporated into the colleges of education. As already noted, the kind of philosophy established within education by the early 1960s led Peters to claim that most philosophers were appalled by what they found. Similarly, it might be worthwhile to pay brief attenton to the fate of psychology as it was introduced into the colleges. Again there is clear evidence that psychology was incorporated into generalised education courses and that the emphasis was placed upon practical considerations rather than theoretical issues and that such an approach drew heavily upon the work related to 'social problems', deviance and established classroom practice.[11] Thus, as psychology has been introduced into the colleges of education, it has taken a special form which in many aspects differs from the nature of theory and research in the over-all discipline. It seems possible to argue, therefore, that as sociology has appeared in the colleges and departments of education, it too has been transformed and transmitted in a unique form. It is important that the selection, organisation and institutionalisation of sociological knowledge within the specific context of the conditions of the colleges and departments be explained.

In general, therefore, I am arguing that there are certain common features of the employment of philosophy, psychology and sociology within teacher education. These features relate to the ideological qualities which, historically, have underpinned the training of teachers. In essence, these ideologies have served to emphasise the affective and non-cognitive aspects of the teacher's task. Well into this century the denominational influence upon the colleges was overwhelming, and Jean Floud's image of the 'missionary spirit' which characterised the colleges is a powerful and accurate one. More recently the secularisation of teacher education has only served to transform the religious ethic of the colleges into an ideology which draws heavily upon romantic concepts of innocence and childhood. As Taylor has indicated, 'the literature of teacher education is replete with statements that emphasise this value orientation'.[12] Taylor draws attention to some of the features which characterise these orientations. He points out the domination of child-centred ideologies in teacher education and the ways in which these ideologies differ from those of the professional practising teacher. Following Parsons he argues that there is a tendency in college courses to emphasise expressive rather than instrumental activity which in turn reflects progressive educational ideology with its emphasis upon education as a part of life rather than as a preparation for life. In turn, this leads readily to a distrust of 'intellect', which is well reflected in the synthetic view held of educational studies. As one member of a college staff has put it, 'education tutors ought to venture into many fields to attempt a synthesis, rather than parcel out the Education course to a collection of "experts" '.[13]

A further consequence of these approaches is that discussions in teacher education frequently incorporate an interest in 'the fundamental goals of life', and, as Taylor has remarked, an 'element of hortatory transcendentalism is a feature of a good deal of the discussions'.[14] In this way the mixture of interpersonal, child-centred concepts of education merge with affective and expressive concern over the nature of education to give rise to a special view of the nature of social change and of the wider society. As Taylor and the earlier discussion of the development of sociology have shown, the teaching in colleges is not really concerned with the major structural and economic features of society or with changes in them. Rather it concentrates on what are issues selected from a very theoretically restricted but pragmatically diverse view of the nature of social change – the effects of technology and dehumanisation, the decline of religion, the welfare state, the problems of the environment, advertising and the mass media. In a similar fashion, discussions on the nature of society and of social change are frequently characterised by a rural nostalgia which can attribute ill to industrialisation and urbanisation by cross reference to the widely held romantic view of childhood as innocence and the child as victim. One result

33

of this is that what is regarded as evidence by educationalists is frequently an insubstantial and vague selection of information and prescription designed to bolster a stated point of view. As Etzioni bitingly remarks of Silberman's influential book, *Crisis in the Classroom* (New York: Random House, 1970), 'Ideas fly cheaply, evidence is hard to muster.'[15] It is clear, moreover, from American discussions that the ideological basis of American teacher education is remarkably similar. Both Bressler[16] and Hansen[17] argue that the ideology or conventional wisdom of education does not readily encourage free, scientific enquiry, as they manifest the characteristics of dogma and faith. In Bressler's own words, 'in the conventional wisdom of education truth and wish are one'.[18]

Moreover, as might be expected these ideological elements both represent and are expressed by certain structural features of the colleges. The very great majority of college-of-education staff in Britain are recruited directly from schools after years of schoolteaching experience. Any attempt to modify these arrangements usually brings strong protests, especially from the teachers' unions, which have urged that no one should be appointed to a college of education post without at least five years' schoolteaching experience. Two consequences have followed from this. First, it is extremely difficult for the educationalist to develop a serious grounding in the basic requirements of educational research. The normal career line hardly allows for it. In teacher training, therefore, those subjects which are not widely taught in the schools, like sociology and psychology, were likely on their introduction to be entrusted to lecturers who were appointed primarily because of their schoolteaching experience in fields other than these core disciplines. It is not without reason, therefore, that the McNair Report noted that the colleges of education 'have never ranked in the public mind as institutions which have a duty as regards the promotion of research and investigation in the field of education'.[19] The second consequence of the emphasis given to practical experience in teacher education is that those engaged in it are likely to have an action orientation. As Bressler has argued, the lecturer's own appointment has been made on the basis of his presumed excellence in teaching; it is difficult, therefore, for him to appear less

34

enthusiastic and committed about his own teaching than he is proposing his students be about their own. This commitment to teaching is, Bressler suggests, likely to make educationalists impatient with the whole business of research which is informed by the perspectives and methods of the social sciences.

It is in a discussion of the position of the education department that the organisational and structural features of teacher education take on their greatest significance for the present argument. Historically, the education departments have developed responsibility for matters pertaining to teaching, whilst the specialist departments have taught the conventional academic school subjects which the students will require in their careers, for example, geography, English or mathematics. Over time, therefore, with the increasing 'professionalisation' of teacher training and the growing efforts to provide it with a more theoretical base, the education department has acquired responsibility for subjects like psychology and sociology. Nevertheless, within the context of the existing structure of personnel, policies have been adopted which relate the professional preparation of teachers 'as closely as possible to the demands that will be made on them in the classroom'.[20] In this way 'the demands' of the classroom are treated as given and unproblematic, and the emphasis is placed on the development of the kind of sociology, psychology and philosophy which have been briefly described. The argument is, therefore, that as has been shown, the ideologies of teacher education, both religious and secular, have interpenetrated the teaching of those disciplines relevant to the study of education. Recent attempts to introduce different, more independent paradigms of academic study have had only partial success. Moreover, it is suggested that this interpenetration is reflected particularly in philosophy and psychology, as well as sociology. It is a general feature and its investigation would seem to be a legitimate area of enquiry for the sociology of knowledge. In this exploratory discussion, attention has been drawn to certain important features of the kind that have led Hansen to note that

the critical stance necessary to productive objectivity . . . appears noticeably tentative in many departments of education. Ideas are readily reduced to practicalities, they are judged for their utility rather than their validity, and in the process, utility becomes the validation, thereby limiting discussion to immediate possibilites or even probabilities and proportionately hobbling creative imagination.[21]

This examination of the structure and ideology of teacher education has helped to show that the general arguments of Bressler and Brim can be supported by reference to the specific development of the professional preparation of teachers. As sociology of education was introduced into the colleges during the 1960s, it was absorbed into a particular ideological and structural context which powerfully influenced the selection of topics for the syllabus and the pedagogic presentation of the subject. Sociology of education has largely been taught within education departments and as such, therefore, it has been exposed to the non-specialist, action perspective of the staff of those departments, for whom, Bressler has observed, 'science is an honoured symbol, but experience becomes the actual basis of knowledge'.[22]

It follows that educationalists will tend to take from sociology what suits them and be distrustful of the rest. Emphasis, therefore, upon such areas as social problems, deviancy, disadvantaged children, the influence of advertising and violence on television can readily be incorporated into an experiential, action perspective. In this way the educationalist can 'shop around' within the field of sociology choosing those topics which deal with 'critical' educational issues, those which can be seen to relate to a human set of values and which might, through the nature of the research findings, offer apparently clear recommendations for action. In this way the construction of the syllabus for the sociology of education which has already been elaborated can be understood, as can the rejection of those parts of sociology (theory, conflict, research methods) which cannot be readily adjusted to the prevailing ethos and can, therefore, be dismissed as not relevant or too technical.

The consequences of this argument will be developed later, but for the moment it is important to understand that certain specific features have enabled and facilitated the conjunction of the two perspectives. Essentially the normative strands in educational studies have emphasised cohesion and integration. Hence it has been possible to describe the syllabuses as attempts to deal with critical social problems. In many respects, however, the sociological parts of education courses have been underpinned by a simple functionalism which has supported straightforward consensual attitudes. Gouldner has, in another context, put the issue well :

> sociological Functionalism's emphasis on the role of moral values and on the significance of morality more generally, often leads it to locate contemporary social problems in the breakdown of the moral system; for example, as due to defects in the systems of socialisation and as due to their failure to train people to behave in conformity with the moral norm. . . . Moral conceptions of social problems may lead to new programs of education or training.[23]

It is not surprising, therefore, that a sociology based on functionalism should be readily adaptable by educationalists. Both this kind of sociology, and education, incorporate certain unstated assumptions, notably that industrial societies are characterised by increasing equality and increasing economic efficiency.

The relationship between sociology and education, therefore, is, in Hansen's terms, 'uncomfortable'. This does not mean, however, that discussion should concentrate purely on the negative aspects of the relationship, but rather that the delicate and interpenetrative elements should be explored. Now, what has made possible the constant links between education and sociology has been, as Gouldner is close to implying, the common ground of discussion of moral values and socialisation. And this has been made possible because of the dominance within sociology of perspectives of structural-functionalism. Over time, educationalists' concern for human betterment, and their belief in the part played by education in achieving social justice and equality of opportunity, has come to be closely associated with largely unexamined assertions about the continuing economic growth and efficiency of Western societies. It is these latter assertions which have, to some degree, underpinned the perspectives of the structural-functionalists. The ideologies of education, with

37

their essentially consensual and reformist features deriving from the Christian and romantic nineteenth-century traditions, are not threatened by a science which points out how the social arrangements can be 'improved' and which offers suitable cues to action. More especially is this likely to be the case when there is the confidence of perceived affluence and the certainties of sustained economic growth.

To the degree, therefore, that sociology and education exist in the form described, it is possible to see the ways in which the selective use made by educationalists of sociology can be explained. There is a real sense in which the dominant tradition of structural-functionalism and the conventional study of education can coexist in an institutional context designed for the preparation of teachers. This is particularly true if this preparation is for a specific kind of school organisation and undertaken by staff who themselves have had the kind of socialisation and induction already noted. The central features of their differences revolve round the place of empirical enquiry. Indeed Hansen has argued that what distinguishes the disciplines of education and sociology is the distinction between normative enquiry and empirical enquiry. Yet what enables them to coexist is the way in which empirical enquiry in the field of education is suffused with normative dimensions. Thus Mays has been congratulated by a notable educationalist precisely because his work is 'thick with value judgments. It is expressive of the kind of society Dr. Mays would like to see.'[24]

The problems of the relationship between the two perspectives are not new. The essential differences are that normative thought and enquiry are addressed to the establishment of imperatives – programmes of action which can be placed within an over-all system of prescription. Empirical enquiry, on the other hand, is dedicated to the establishment of knowledge which is deemed to be independently verified and which can lead to descriptions of the nature of reality, which is presumed to exist. Sociologists, generally, have been aware of these distinctions and of the possible confusions which might arise. To some degree they have been forced to do so by the long-standing survival of alternative views of the nature of the discipline which have persistently challenged the dominant assumptions of the modes of enquiry

38

developed by the empiricists. In education, however, the issues are less well discussed and defined. It is possible that this may be because of the way in which educationalists have adopted the research techniques of the empirical mood without noting, as it were, the spirit of the form. What frequently happens, therefore, is that educational research succeeds in utilising and manipulating technical apparatus to demonstrate an essentially normative position. It is this problem which underlies the whole standing of much educational research.

In many respects the situation is the complete opposite to that which many of the recent critics of the sociology of education suppose. To accuse the sociologists of education of steering clear of social and political debate is to largely miss the point. The major characteristics, over a long period, of the sociology of education as it has been practised has been the commitment of the practitioners to certain types of social and educational change. Moreover, the work of the sociologists of education has made some impact at the level of policy.

The normative doctrines of the educationalists, heavily characterised by the desire to change the world, have, as has been shown, found expression in the organisational and pedagogic arrangements within colleges and departments of education. The perspectives of the educationalists have therefore dominated the selection of teaching topics and the contexts in which they have been presented. Moreover, the strong reformist origins of research in the sociology of education have provided the educationalist with a series of 'topics' which have suited them well, and from which it has been easy to omit areas of study which have not suited the relevant ideologies.

This dialectic between the sociologists and the educationalists has largely been conducted on the educationalists' terms because the teaching of the sociology of education has taken place within institutions ostensibly devoted to the preparation of teachers and educational administrators. These institutions have to face the continual demands for immediate research and theory which can be deemed useful to practitioners. In this fashion, 'theory' can readily become concerned with what is regarded as 'efficiency', and a place can be found for the 'wisdom of experience' with which the educationalists so strongly bolster their position. Similarly, a recent President of the National Union of Teachers has felt moved to assert that sociologists and psychologists

> do not know the problems of the classroom. [Teachers] need to be reassured that many who are concerned in research have been teachers and know the problems of the classroom. They need to be able to see that the results of the research can be written in such a way that the understanding of the teacher's problem is not excluded in the profusion of evidence and conclusions.[25]

The tension between the two disciplines can be seen at its most noticeable when sociology appears as an abstracting or generalising discipline and education as a predictive or hortatory one. As has already been suggested, this can readily mean that the educator is frustrated in finding application for the sociologist's findings, and the sociologist is bitter that the educationalist is unable to evaluate his work. This tension between practice, theory and research in the field of education is excellently illustrated by the way in which the sociological research of Bernstein has been handled in an educational context over the last fifteen years.[26] To begin with, it was taken into the educationalist context by providing an explanation for working-class achievement within the educational system. Bernstein's ideas became widely diffused throughout the early 1960s, since they apparently provided an indictment of the class system and could readily encourage the notion of the child as victim of the process of socialisation. As the work developed, however, an increasing degree of technical expertise was required to interpret the empirical findings, and the consequent theoretical development of Bernstein's ideas only served to generalise and make more sophisticated his conceptual framework. Thus, by the early 1970s Bernstein's work was heavily under attack by many educationalists who argued that he had a 'deficit' model of the working class and that he was viewing the working class from a middle-class perspective.[27] The significant point in terms of the present argument, however, is to note that at both stages the response to Bernstein's work has been largely ideological, indeed political. What really changed between the 1950s and the 1970s

40

was the ideological and political context of the practice of education.

Thus far, there has been an attempt to explain the kind of sociology of education we have in terms of certain independent factors. Attention has been drawn to the dominance of functionalist theories in sociology and the ways in which these have affected the sociology of education. In the period of perceived affluence and educational expansion, the practice of the sociologists of education was informed by a commitment to social justice and economic efficiency which were not seen as being mutually exclusive. Rather they were twin desirable goals, meaningful to reformers as representing the changing direction of society as against older elitist notions. Moreover, it has been shown that the nature of the sociologists' commitment powerfully influenced the choice of research topics and the presentation of research findings, and also that the commitment of the sociologists was not totally irrelevant at the level of political action. In essence, the conventional practice of the sociology of education has been optimistic and reformist, a perspective which has suited admirably the normative ethos of the colleges of education. Critique has gone hand in hand with remedy, and the consequences of this have undoubtedly been found in some of the educational changes which various governments have introduced.

Essentially what has changed this situation and brought about the 'new' sociology of education has been the growing realisation of the inefficacy of remedy. This has taken a variety of different forms. At one level it is possible to note the retreat from functionalism. This retreat was manifest in the active pursuit of alternative perspectives not only at the level of private and individual research but also in the collective actions of sociologists at various national and international conferences throughout the late 1960s and early 1970s. Equally significant, as Gouldner has pointed out, is the emergence of radically novel and over-arching theoretical models whose underlying assumptions and basic assertions differ vitally from those of functionalism. Altogether, there is a widespread feeling of uneasiness at the lack of certainty and clarity regarding the theoretical foundations of sociology. This can be seen in the emergence of diverse theoretical perspectives which emphasise the ways in which men create their social world – social

41

dramaturgy, phenomenology, ethnomethodology and cultural relativism. It is, of course, difficult to be certain why these new perspectives should currently be developed, but anyone concerned with the sociology of knowledge should at least ask questions about genesis and change in the acceptability of social theories. As far as education is concerned, it is relatively easy to trace speculatively the retreat from that earlier optimism. At an individual level the experience of higher education has, it is claimed, not given to those who have undergone it a sense of involvement. Rather the educational process has become too readily defined as a series of hurdles to be jumped on the route to qualifications and personal advancement.

In addition, recently it is possible that even the material rewards have been perceived as less readily available. More importantly, this private experience has been reflected at the public level. The expansion of systems of education as recommended by sociologists and educationalists has only marginally altered the relationship between social class and educational opportunity. Educational reform as presented in the form of comprehensive education, individual instruction or de-streaming has not transformed the educational process, nor altered the relationship of that process to the occupational order. Elsewhere, education has not turned out to be the vehicle for the rapid transformation of the underdeveloped societies. Now if all of this is increasingly apparent at a general and public level, it is partly so because conventional sociological enquiry has shown it to be so. The debate initiated by the sociologists of education has in fact turned in upon itself. Their dialogue has taken on the quality of echoing voices as the prescriptive certainties of the 1950s and 1960s have been examined and found to be full of complexities and unintended consequences. It will be helpful to explore the collapse of the optimism in more detail before examining the response to it.

3. AN ACCOUNT OF THE SOCIOLOGY OF EDUCATION: II

THE analyses of sociologists and their recommendations have been in the direction of expansionist and egalitarian educational policies. As already argued, expansion would facilitate personal opportunity, and so hasten a more just society. Also it would provide more trained, skilled manpower as demanded by the needs of the economy. The 'pool of ability' would be further tapped to provide personal and public advantage. At the same time, interventionist programmes could assist those whose social environment did not facilitate educational opportunity and educational success. In many Western societies a great deal of the publicised educational efforts of the 1960s was devoted to policies which would implement such purposes. Yet, by now, there is a disillusionment with such policies and a growing questioning by sociologists of the basis on which they have been established. The expansion of systems of higher education and the proliferation of qualifications have not readily brought greater equality, nor have existing elite groups been challenged by those with new educational qualifications. As Giddens has noted,

> the educational qualifications associated with recruitment to elite groupings still tend to be very much those associated with a background of material privilege. What influences elite recruitment is not that the aspirant possesses a degree in physics or in engineering, but that the degree is conferred at Oxford or at Harvard . . . it is everywhere true that ownership of wealth and property continues to play a fundamental part in facilitating access to the sort of educational process which influences entry to elite positions.[1]

In their different ways, Collins and Berg also have shown that the benefits to be obtained from education are not what have frequently been claimed. Collins has argued that the educational requirements for employment are an index of employers' determination to recruit socially acceptable and adequately socialised employees. Collins argues that the 'higher the normative control concerns of the employer, and the more elite the organisation's status, the higher his educational requirements'.[2] Collins therefore challenges the technical-function theory of education and argues that the main activity of schools is to teach particular status culture, and that this might be associated with the kinds of control maintained within work organisations. Berg[3] suggests that there is little evidence that employers need to raise educational standards in the interests of efficiency. Indeed, by establishing that educational qualifications come to be used as a screening device which functions to confine large numbers of people to low-skill, no-opportunity jobs, Berg challenges the whole basis of the kind of expansion of higher education which has taken place in the United States.

It is not only, however, in respect of elite recruitment that the simple benefits of educational qualifications are questioned. There is increasing discussion of the view that the importance of education has been overestimated in raising individual income, or in making significant contributions to the more general features of social mobility, and even in raising the productivity, that is the efficiency, of the labour force. At the same time, the benefits of educational interventionist programmes to improve the position of the children of the poor have been challenged by work undertaken by social scientists.

This decline in the belief in the efficacy of educational expansion at a societal level has its parallel in Britain in the growing realisation of the problems associated with specific educational reforms. Thus, Ford[4] has questioned the degree to which comprehensive schools can achieve the optimistic objectives of those who have so vociferously proposed them. Barker-Lunn[5] has shown that de-streaming does not transform the educational performance of working-class children in primary schools. At the same time, other studies have shown that a variety of educational innovations which have been generally recommended on the grounds that they will improve the learning of pupils, particularly working-class pupils, have been shown not to work in the fashion prescribed.

It is impossible here to explore in detail all of the most recent work which has challenged the conventional wisdom of the educationalists and the sociologists of education. Nor is it important, at this stage, to consider the technical and analytical validity of those studies which have changed opinion. For the moment it is sufficient that they exist. Foremost amongst those who have challenged the dominant liberal dogmas of an expansionist and egalitarian educational system is Jencks. Jencks spent the years from 1961–7 in Washington, and has explained his purposes in writing his book *Inequality* thus : 'I left Washington convinced that the liberal social reforms of the 1960's had been seriously misdirected. I also felt that this could be at least partly traced to the fact that federal policy-makers and legislators had more or less accepted a series of plausible but erroneous assumptions about the nature of poverty and inequality in America.'[6]

Jencks notes that these assumptions can be briefly stated. Eliminating poverty is largely a matter of helping children born into poverty to rise out of it. Children of poor parents find it difficult to escape from poverty because they do not acquire the basic cognitive skills and are consequently disadvantaged in the labour market. The best way of solving this problem is educational reform. Thus the children of the poor must be taught their skills at school, if necessary by making sure that they attend the same schools as middle-class children or have compensatory programmes. As a result of his own and his associates' work, however, Jencks concludes that

> many popular explanations of economic inequality are largely wrong. We cannot blame economic inequality primarily on genetic differences in men's capacity for abstract reasoning, since there is nearly as much economic inequality among men with equal test scores as among men in general. We cannot blame economic inequality primarily on the fact that parents pass along their disadvantages to their children, since there is nearly as much inequality among men whose parents had the same economic status as among men in general. We cannot blame economic inequality on differences between schools, since differences between schools seem to have very little effect on any measurable attribute to those who attend them.[7]

Now what is important about Jencks's work is that it challenges so many of the conventionally held beliefs. As Miller neatly puts it, 'It was disaster throughout the 60's – and it is an endemic disease of liberal thought – to defend what is desired for its own sake on the grounds that it is instrumental for something else.'[8] Moreover, although Jencks's work was not published until 1972, it reflected a growing awareness of the possibility that too much has been expected of education. The relative failure of the various interventionist programmes specifically designed to help the poor and the black was already being documented by the late 1960s, and by 1969 had formed the starting point of Jensen's re-assertion of the genetic factors in educational performance.

The challenge to the prevailing, largely progressive and liberal orthodoxies which has been implicit in much recent work has brought forth a variety of significant responses. One has already been noted – the re-emergence of psychological theories of intelligence which stress genetic endowment. The apparent failure of policies which essentially manipulate resources, the environment, the school organisation and the teaching styles has led many to an increasing belief that the genetic make-up of the pupil is the vital factor. The quality of the debate over the views of those like Jensen,[9] Eysenck[10] and Herrnstein[11] who have been the forerunner in re-establishing psychologicalgenetic theories shows clearly the ideological quality of much that passes for research in education.

Even more novel has been the response which has challenged the whole notion of compulsory schooling as it has developed in the nineteenth and twentieth centuries. The various advocates of de-schooling and free schooling choose to see compulsory education as having no real functions other than those of oppression and subjugation. Those who adopt this position frequently incorporate into their ideas notions of the relativity of knowledge which enables them to attack conventional schooling in terms of the ways in which it imposes middle-class views of the world on essentially unwilling working-class pupils.

Such perspectives can find theoretical support in the response from which this study began – the view that the sociology of education should be as the sociology of knowledge. Arguments

46

of this kind, as has already been shown, make it possible to provide a strong theoretical critique of many of the early studies, to develop a new style and method of enquiry and to advocate a new area of enquiry – the school curriculum.

The emergence of this new view of the sociology of education is remarkable, however, not so much for its self-claimed novelty, as for its manifestation of many of the significant features of the sociological study of educational systems which have already been described. First, it matches well with changes in educational ideologies and advanced school practice and so maintains the incorporation of the supposedly 'tough' discipline in a normative framework manageable by educationalists. Second, it is little more than the synthetic joining of a number of trends which have been manifest in recent changes in academic sociology. If the sociology of education of the 1950s and 1960s reflected the ideologies underpinning academic sociology on the one hand, and recommended school practice on the other, then the new sociology of education might similarly be interpreted as a reflection of the newer academic ideologies and the more recently advocated practice.

There is a very real sense in which the new developments in the sociology of education can therefore be seen as relating to the supposed 'crisis' in sociology. Giddens, however, has argued that there is not so much a crisis but rather evidence of a transitionary phase in social theory.[12] He suggests that certain recent developments in Western societies – France 1968, student radicalism, increasing strike levels, internal political disturbance and militancy – can be seen as presenting a challenge to the comfortable 'consensus politics' which have characterised the last twenty years. This apparent increase in social and political disturbance cannot, moreover, be readily explained by the dominant theories of academic sociology, that is those of structural-functionalism. Giddens has noted four theoretical responses in academic sociology, each departing from the premises of structural-functionalism and incorporating, to some degree, elements of Marxist thought. It is important to recognise, however, that if Giddens's analysis is acceptable, then it has clear implications for any explanation of the recent developments in the sociology of education.

Giddens points out that the first challenge to those who have upheld the perpectives of structural-functionalism originates with the supporters of 'conflict theory'. It is claimed that structural-functionalism gives an inadequate account of the origins of social order because it fails to take sufficient account of differing interests originating in the sectional divisions within society as a whole. Within education, Collins's arguments have already been noted and further support for this point of view is to be found in a diverse variety of radical educational authors.

A second perspective, frequently linked with 'conflict theory', though in fact different from it, seeks to contrast 'conservative' and 'radical' sociology. In essence this remains an ideological debate and hence is reflected in discussions about education. It is argued that structural-functionalism is conservative, and that its deficiencies and its political implications can be exposed by a radical perspective. Arguments of this kind have been well developed by Holly[13] and also find support in the writing of Keddie[14] and the Rosens.[15] The over-all result, however, is exemplified in much current educational discussion. In general it leads to competing ideological interpretations of social reality, and, especially in education, to much confusion as to where the radical advocates stand in relation to the material they are studying.

Third, the decline in the meaningfulness of structural-functionalism has encouraged a variety of anthropomorphic theories which relegate the importance of institutional analysis in favour of emphasising the significance of 'everyday life'. This microsociological approach tends to ignore the structural problems which have exercised the sociological imagination for the last 100 years and to emphasise an approach which elevates the individual and his special interpretation of reality. Again, in education such change has proved very attractive. First, it apparently allows the pupils' perspective to be treated in an equivalent fashion to that of the educator and teacher, and, second, it provides legitimation for the increase in classroom studies which began in an atheoretical fashion and which can make claim to much greater 'relevance' than other kinds of sociological research in the field of education.

The final response to the current crisis in sociology, and one which incorporates some measure of the previous three, is the move to the sociology of knowledge. In some respects it can be seen as solving the problems of making distinctions between ideologies and knowledge, and placing its advocates in a strong position to attack the value-free or neutral aspects of structural-functionalism with which current critics are so concerned. In education, also, it opens the door to the sociology of the curriculum, as the school curriculum clearly embraces a variety of forms of knowledge. As has been shown, the recent work of Young began by urging that the sociology of education should be part of the sociology of knowledge. For Young this would also contribute to the development of social theory. Yet given the oft-stated logical difficulties involved in this kind of relativism, it seems unlikely that moving the sociology of education towards the sociology of knowledge will bring about a new theoretical framework for sociology. Indeed, one of the most notable features of Young's attempts to move the sociology of education towards the sociology of knowledge is his failure to consider, in his major contribution, *Knowledge and Control*, the conventional arguments against such an approach. It is only in later, short articles that Young seriously attempts to deal with the frequently argued objections to the general principles which underlie his position. These objections imply that if Young is arguing in favour of the relativism of knowledge and theories about knowledge, relativism of a cultural and historical kind, then the same accusation can be made about his own knowledge. Young's more recent response to such criticism is, he acknowledges, tentative. He agrees that he does wish to discuss the problem of relativism which he describes as arising from the view that 'if all knowledge is a social and historical product, then we have no grounds for deciding the worth, truth or value of anything'.[16] Young asserts, however, that this should not lead to the despair frequently associated with relativism. In its place Young offers the sociology of knowledge imbued with commitment and an understanding of common humanity. In order to assert these characteristics of the sociology of knowledge. Young develops the notion of 're-flexive sociology' proposed by O'Neill.[17] The commitment to re-flexivity will involve the sociologist in attempting to provide the grounds for his own sociological activity. In this fashion, commitment will involve a recognition of differing perspectives, and theory and research need no longer be separate. As Young notes, 'then commitment to our perspective rather than another seems not only necessary but inescapable'.[18] According to these arguments, therefore, reflexivity is a prescriptive feature of the sociological method. In turn, sociological accounts cannot be viewed as manifesting a hierarchy of adequacy, rather they are just other versions of reality that are offered by sociologists. It follows, therefore, that Young is not attracted by the tradition of the sociology of knowledge deriving from Scheler and Mannheim. This tradition embodies distinctive writing analysing the social character of knowledge. It is not, however, reflexive about its own activity, and therefore does not treat the sociology of knowledge as social.

As already suggested, it is tempting to view these most recent developments in Young's work as a result of the original omissions in his discussion of the issues concerning the nature and growth of knowledge. There is a very real sense in which the revision of his ideas has been consequential upon criticism and discussion of the original formulations and, in particular, of his failure to face fully the implications of a relativist position with respect to the epistemological issues and criteria for truth in a variety of different disciplines. Thus Young regards the sociology of knowledge as not being distinct from sociology, in the sense that all sociolgy is a sociology of knowledge. He can, therefore, go on to argue that notions of everyday, common-sense or tacit knowledge, the knowledge that we draw on whatever we are doing, are not then viewed as distinct from the formalised bodies of knowledge such as philosophy, science, and literature. Similarly, therefore, Young can assert that the 'findings' of sociologists which purport to prove, describe, show, and explain are merely political facts of life not related to the unique methods of 'doing' sociology.

It is this over-all standpoint which enables Young to adopt the sociological perspectives of O'Neill and Douglas. He writes, for example, 'It is possible, therefore, that the "crutches" offered by "objectivist" theories of knowledge may be seen as an attempt to evade something fundamental like being a person, historically and socially situated, and as such oneself, responsible.'[19] Despite the obscurantist tone of this statement, Young seems to mean that sociologists of education will offer teachers the opportunity of rejecting any assumptions of the superiority of educational or 'academic' knowledge over the everyday common-sense knowledge available to people as being in the world. It is in this way, therefore, that Young can support a view of sociology as the subversion of absolutism and can press the point that what is required of sociology is that it should ask questions about the superiority of sociological knowledge with a view not only to interpreting the world but also to changing it.

The over-all position, however, contains many problematical elements. To a large degree it only compounds the uncertainties which existed in the original arguments. Most especially, the standpoint advocated by Young makes it hard to explore the differences between different forms of knowledge. As such, therefore, Young too readily side-steps important philosophical and epistemological questions concerning the nature of belief, ideology and knowledge, and, also, too many sociological questions associated with the nature of rationality.

It is, of course, interesting to compare Young's arguments with those of Burns, and also with the analysis developed by Kogan. Both emphasise the way that the sociologists of education have indeed 'changed the world', or at least a portion of it. Young, however, does not recognise these kind of changes, nor, seemingly, the commitment of the early sociologists of education, or the over-all commitment of the normative ideological framework in which sociological studies are conducted. Indeed, his solution to the whole problem raised by the assertion of the relativism of knowledge is 'a project which does not divorce sociological enquiry from political action'.[20] In this way Young has arrived at an old dilemma – uncertain as many have been before, whether social science offers an empirically verified set of theories or a guide to political action – he chooses to opt for both.

Thus, he argues that all methods, pragmatic, Marxist, scientific or formal, have the 'defect' that they have to be used and 'only take on their meaning in the context of their use', and 'that the problems of validity of truth criteria or relativism in the sociology of knowledge are still evaded rather than confronted, whether one turns to one of a variety of objectivistic views of knowledge,

51

to Dewey's "rational man" . . . Weber's "rational actor" or to Marx's proletariat'.[21] The solution, advocated by Young, to these difficulties is to turn to the work of Merleau-Ponty.[22] Taking Merleau-Ponty's idea that 'we have to work without certainty "in confusion towards truth" ',[23] Young argues that this can be seen as the centre of the kind of dilemmas he has raised by his epistemological discussion. Young accepts Merleau-Ponty's notions that the central characteristics of human life are violence and uncertainty, but that these only become apparent at certain critical times such as conquest or revolution. At those times men have to choose and take the consequences. Paradoxically, however, although these are the fundamental qualities of history and social life, Young is still happy to assert that 'it is usually possible to live life as if they were not'.[24] The significance of this kind of approach for Young is that, in his terms, it enables him to resolve some of the dilemmas of relativism which have become increasingly apparent as the debate about his work has continued. The risks and contingencies to which Merleau-Ponty refers arise from a recognition of the partial and limited perceptions on which we act. These perceptions take on the characteristics of absolutes for individuals, and though they are limited both socially and historically, they become the only grounds individuals have for action. Thus the relativism on human grounds becomes as absolute that implies an understanding that whatever one undertakes involves commitment, the risk of failure and disillusion, whatever the intentions might be. Clearly, this kind of absolutism is different from the certainty provided by an external agency or rule system. Events, then, are how they are interpreted and knowledge is, at best, a guide. Action is decision to 'insert ourselves into the course of events'.[25] It follows that all action can be seen as being at risk, and that the academic spectator who is just reviewing the commitments of others is guilty of bad faith. Young, therefore, takes as his cue Merleau-Ponty's description of the French resistance fighters as 'taking sides against the probable'. This must be seen in comparison to much of our social life which is concerned with 'living with the probable', and much of our social science, concerned as it is with discovering the probable. Young concludes that

Some of the confusion and quite justifiable antagonism felt by practitioners such as teachers towards sociologists might be removed if both realised they shared a common human history, and that often categories such as 'teacher' and 'sociologist', while appearing to protect them as persons, in effect often prevent the possibility of their so being . . . in the end personal commitments . . . are grounds for action, whether that action is deciding what to do in the classroom or 'the adequacy' of a researcher's account. The point then is not to ask whether particular research methods are, of themselves, 'good' or 'bad', but to ask for what and for whom are we providing accounts.[26]

Young's extension of his original argument does not clarify any of the major substantive issues. As already noted, his latter position seems to imply hostility between sociologists and teachers which requires resolution, whereas much of his earlier analysis was based on the assumption that sociologists had too readily accepted the teachers' perspectives and hence failed to 'make' their own problems. Second, Young's newer arguments are surrounded by some degree of mystification. Indeed it is difficult to see how an approach such as he now advocates might appeal to the majority of practising teachers. In his demand for a reflexive sociology, Young seems to be inviting teachers to be involved at the frontiers of a debate in the social sciences which will require a great deal of philosophical sophistication. It is, in fact, tempting to ask of Young 'for what and for whom' is he now providing an account. In turn, it might be possible to conceive of an answer which draws attention to the important issues arising from his neglect of the problems associated with relativism in his original work, whilst at the same time maintaining an appeal to radical educational practitioners amongst whom that work has been well received. For it is precisely commitment, action, and personal experience upon which they base their work in schools.

Moreover, it is possible to argue that the recent alteration in his position, which stresses the humanistic element in his arguments, enables Young to remain effectively within the normative tradition of educational studies, which has already been described. It is a tradition which emphasises uniqueness and individuality and whose practitioners and ideologies have been described above. Finally, it is clear that Young can only adopt the position that he does by choosing to ignore the commitment of the early sociologists of education, and he is driven to this position because he can provide no adequate grounds for choosing between different people's commitments. The ideological elements in Young's own position are perhaps best expressed in his justification of the importance of Merleau-Ponty's ideas for educational theorising. Young argues that Merleau-Ponty's perspective :

> suggests that our joint enterprise . . . the political commitment to engage with others, teachers, parents, students, pupils. . . . And engagement that is as likely to take us out of the confines of the academy as not and beyond the institutions of formal educations as within it . . . it [means] a radicalism towards possibilities of change, whatever the experienced constraints about knowledge, pupils, schools or the economy, that philosophers, sociologists and psychologists tend to have done little more than confirm. If we start to ask what this kind of radicalism means in the contexts we find ourselves, we may also make 'educational theorising' a way of learning to change the world.[27]

The ideological features here are virtually undisguised, and with few amendments Young's observations could serve any conventional ideology of education.

4. CRITIQUE AND CONCLUSION

IN the end, Young's arguments do not allow us to escape from the ideologists of education. 'Changing the world' ignores all the questions concerning the directions of that change. As Banks has commented, the advocates of the 'new' sociology of education tend to adopt 'ideological and indeed political reasons which lead them to reject the post-war sociology of education and indeed a great deal of traditional sociology itself. This has its roots in the strong commitment to . . . an activist as distinct from a passive or determinist approach to man in society.'[1]

In many respects Williamson puts the issues well when he argues that the new sociologists fail in their attempts to redefine the subject because of their uncertainties over the analysis of power and the relationship between the distribution of power and the distribution of knowledge.[2] Thus it might be possible to view the retreat within the sociology of education to the detailed analysis of the mosaic of face-to-face relationships and classroom interaction as one consequence of the inadequacies of the discussion of power and knowledge.

As is increasingly recognised, however, the 'new' sociology of education can provide academic legitimation for politically and ideologically based current educational practice in just the same way as the reformist sociology of the last quarter of a century has done for piecemeal administrative and organisational change. There is a sense in which Young might now recognise this.[3] Certainly the point is well made by Banks when she highlights the problems of 'activist' ideologies advocated by Keddie, and can be briefly illustrated by reference to some of the recommended practices and their underlying ideologies in the teaching of English in schools.

In English teaching many of the innovative practices involve challenging the more conventional aspects of the subject, notably the literary tradition; both in terms of the written word and in terms of the notion of great literature. These elements in English are decried because they can be used by the teacher to impose an alien middle-class culture upon unwilling working-class pupils, and thereby serve to undermine or deny the culture of those pupils and indeed to challenge their whole sense of identity. Rosen and Searle are amongst the foremost advocates of the new approaches to English teaching. Searle attacks the 'syllabus of established middle class culture' and urges that 'we must re-establish culture in its organic democratic sense'.[4] Moreover, he argues that 'the teacher of English must stand up and affirm the working class loyalties of the language that his students speak . . . [and] move towards establishing criteria developed through the culture of their own social class and belongingness'.[5] The prescriptive and ideological features of this argument can be readily supported by reference to a sociology of education which emphasises personal accounts and the close association of knowledge and power. Rosen is explicit in using the work of the new sociologists of education to legitimise his attack upon the written tradition; he writes,

As Michael Young has pointed out those activities which are mediated by writing and books are accorded special prestige, and no theory of the curriculum can escape this fact. . . . Writing began as the monopoly of a privileged class, and in our own day books are written which surround their contents with all kinds of linguistic mystification. The world of books and writing is not a free-wheeling democratic teach-in.[6]

In exactly the same way, Clark explores and advocates the political significance of the new English teaching, whilst, perhaps unwittingly, placing himself firmly within the traditional ideologies of education. 'It is wrong', he writes,

to speak of 'a change of teaching method' when a moment's reflection persuades us that what we are involved in is nothing less than a revolution in social relations in the English classroom and to a lesser extent within the total institutions we work in . . . the shift from prescriptive English teaching to an expressionistic approach has been accompanied by a shift from a regulative teaching style to a much more permissive and egalitarian one.[7]

Once again it is possible to argue that those who urge the establishment of egalitarian classroom relations can readily draw support from a sociology of education which challenges the basis of 'expert' knowledge and sees the knowledge of the teacher as his means of subjugating pupils.

Confirmation of the possibility that the new sociology of education legitimises certain teaching styles and curricula strategies can be found in the anxieties expressed by both Yardley and Whitty. Yardley, writing with long practical experience of comprehensive schools, warns that the recent advocates of change in the sociology of education devalue 'the work of countless teachers in thousands of our schools'[8] by insisting that what occurs to teachers in training is more humanist than the influences to be' found in schools. Yardley points out that teachers might be suspicious 'of theories which, like the "new direction", might be taken to imply the sanctioning of relaxation of academic rigour and the pursuit of a "soft" line with the less responsive part of the class'.[9]

Whitty makes a similar point when he expresses the fear that, amongst recent graduates in sociology, 'a relativistic view of knowledge and the rejection of the superiority of an academic curriculum has led to fear of imposing any mode of thinking upon pupils and hence to a teaching strategy of "having a chat" '. Indeed, Whitty pointedly notes that the new sociology of education should 'beware of treading too far along the path . . . which verges on a romantic individualism'.[10]

Nor is it only in classroom practice that the new sociology of education might serve to legitimise and promote one kind of educational ideology at the expense of another. There are clear implications for what counts as educational research. This is shown by the Rosens in their 'Introduction' to the Schools Council Project on 'Language Development in the Primary School'. As already suggested, the Rosens are both advocates of the new methods of English teaching in schools and major critics of research in the traditional sociology of education and its treatment of the working class. They write of their own project that,

Readers will have been quick to note that the project plan did not call for anything which could be dignified by the name of research. . . . No elegant design and meticulous execution. No tables of statistics. No explicit hypotheses rigorously tested. No sampling. No control groups. No orderly summary of findings. Anyone expecting such things should turn elsewhere.[11]

It should be noted, in assessing such statements, that those who advocate them are also amongst those who ask us to give the most weight to the symbolic and implicit meanings of language.

It is not surprising, therefore, that these developments have been criticised. Shipman,[12] for example, has been critical of the newer phenomenological perspectives in the sociology of education because they treat as unproblematic the nature of evidence in the social sciences, and Banks has pointed out that assertion frequently takes the place of evidence. In this very important sense, the advocates of the new sociology fail to face important problems regarding their stand relative to the material they are studying, and so remain very much within the normative tradition of educational ideologies which have been described earlier. These ideologies treat as unimportant debates about the nature and limitations of evidence, but allow humane and individualistic perspectives to dominate, and millennial solutions to remain always possible. Moreover, the new sociology of education, by drawing upon changes in sociological theory which emphasise man as 'active' in society, provides legitimation not only for much current educational practice and its associated ideologies, but also for the long-standing activist, experiential tradition in educational studies which have been described earlier.

Thus the new ideas implicit in recent developments within the sociology of education can be understood in the same general terms as those which I have used to explain the conventional sociology of education. As I have argued, the growth of the sociology of education in post-war Britain can best be viewed in the context of its relationships to the dominant sociological theories of structural-functionalism, to the expansionist changes in educational policy which represented a concern for social justice and economic efficiency, and to the basically humane, progressive and individualistic ideologies of teacher education. Similarly, to interpret the new sociology of education it is necessary to understand the background of recent and related developments : the changed mood within sociological theory, which is increasingly philosophical and personal; the uncertainties surrounding the achievements of policies based upon organisational changes designed to bring about radical alterations in social relationships; and, finally, the persistence and extensions of the romantic and individual ideologies of teacher education which have been reinforced by educationalists' too-ready acceptance of the nature of future societies and their democratic base.

In both kinds of sociology of education, I have suggested, ideological elements are to be found. There is, however, an important difference. The old sociology of education contained, also, a commitment on the part of its practitioners to the possibility of arriving at truth. Within the conventional sociology of education, therefore, it is possible to explore the tensions between the ideological elements and the scientific qualities. Indeed, a large part of this book has been devoted to just such an exploration. Within the new sociology of education, and particularly the general sociological standpoints from which it develops, it is very difficult to make the distinction between 'ideology' and 'science'.

In a work of this kind it is impossible to consider in detail all of the arguments connected with the epistemological debate about the nature of knowledge which underlie many of the current issues. Nevertheless, it is important to recognise the fundamental challenge to existing conceptions of knowledge which, say, Esland has made in *Knowledge and Control*. Clearly, if truth and objectivity are to be viewed as human products, and 'reality' is completely dependent upon the meanings and interpretations which men place upon events, then important implications follow for analyses of the nature of knowledge and, by extension, for what might be taught in schools. If, moreover, one argues as Esland does that particular forms of knowledge can best be seen as merely the ideological positions of particular interest groups, and that the acceptability of different epistemologies rests solely upon the legitimating power and abilities of the various institutionalised scholarly groups, then it becomes impossible to make distinctions about the nature of knowledge other than in terms that relate to the organisation and power of those legitimating communities. New knowledge, changed paradigms, are not to be judged by their relevance to an external reality and their accuracy in facilitating a description and an understanding of that reality but in relation to the interests and power of those who create and use the knowledge. Again, it is possible to see the close association between sociologists who adopt these standpoints and who, therefore, readily challenge the absolute and authoritarian elements which might be inherent in accounts of knowledge which emphasise its objective qualities, and radical teachers who are anxious to challenge the authoritarian and hierarchical organisation of much teaching and school organisation.

In the end this leads us back to the central issues. As has been shown, Young's arguments and those of his associates can be treated as representative of the new sociology of education. I have demonstrated how he has moved from a concern with an almost classical view of the sociology of knowledge to one which emphasises commitment and the origins and purposes of analytical accounts. Yet, despite the widespread appeal of such views to educationalists, many important problems remain unresolved.

Thus Young does not explore the nature of commitment. Commitments must involve beliefs which can be examined as true or false. It is a weak and circular argument to propose that there is commitment because of belief in something which can only be true relative to that system of belief. Commitments must be based on beliefs which are external to the system under consideration. The ideas proposed by Young, Esland, and later by Gorbutt,[13] do not recognise this. Moreover, they fail to face the implications of differences in commitment. Not everyone is committed to the same thing. Amongst the many commitments there are differences, some of which may even conflict with each other. How can we decide between them? It is no solution to compare accounts in terms of the degree to which they represent a disposition to change the world. Change itself can be variously interpreted and evaluated.

In the end much of the most recent innovations in the sociology of education fail to come to grips with the important issues arising from discussions of truth and relativism. In so far as advocates of the 'new directions' see their own work in terms of an improvement, progress or an advance on the existing sociology of education, then it is difficult to see why anyone else should accept it as such. There must be some way in which alternative or differing theories can be compared, yet this is precisely what their over-all position would seem to deny, and similarly there must be some criteria by which a 'new' development can be treated as an improvement. In this way the question of what is true in the sociology of education must be treated as central, and consequently the possibility that some people or some statements are wrong must be raised. If the only basis for distinguishing between theories is the personalities of their exponents, the commitment of the individuals or the theories to unspecified change, or the given consensus in professional research, then there appears to be no basis upon which one might make a judgement about different theories. It is impossible to say what 'being wrong' might constitute.

These are amongst some of the unresolved problems in the new sociology of education. Possibly the issues might not merit widespread or general attention if they were confined to a debate about the nature of the sociology of education, or even of the social sciences. As has been shown, however, the advocates of the new perspectives claim also to be writing about the nature of knowledge in general, as well as the specific features of the school curriculum. In doing this, therefore, they are raising epistemological problems in fields far removed from the social sciences and also challenging a wide range of teachers in a fashion which Whitty[14] has usefully analysed. There are already signs that the relativist challenge is being resisted and that some of the initial formulations have been overstated by their advocates. Within the sociology of education alone, Eggleston[15] has attempted a reconciliation of what he sees as competing paradigms, and Williamson[16] has warned against the danger in intellectual innovation that the significance of earlier paradigms of enquiry will be devalued, and that the value and distinctiveness of new approaches will be overestimated. Young[17] has expressed reservations about some of the more extreme versions of the relativist position which have been utilised to atack, say, literacy in schools.

In more general terms there has been opposition to the relativist position on philosophical and epistemological grounds which it is not appropriate to consider in detail here. Suffice to emphasise, once again, that many of the difficulties inherent in much of the recent debate in the sociology of education stem from the absence of any notion of objectivity. Explanations and work in the field are analysed in terms of their ideological stance. In Bernstein's words,

> once the ideological stance is exposed, then all the work may be written off. Every new approach becomes a social movement or sect which immediately defines the nature of the subject by re-defining what is to be admitted, and what is beyond the pale, so that with every new approach the subject almost starts from scratch.[18]

Central to any concluding discussion, therefore, must be a consideration of the issues which relate to the question of truth, objectivity and ideology in the sociology of education, and possibly, by extension, in the wider field of the nature of knowledge. Certain central points can be made and these might be a useful base for considering possible future developments within the sociology of education. Clearly, we are returning to some of the points from which this whole discussion began – the relationship between the genesis of a set of ideas or theories and the degree to which the ideas or theories are worthy of acceptance or rejection.

Discussions of knowledge conducted by philosophers frequently raise questions similar to those posed by Young, but with one notable difference – philosophers concern themselves with attempting to understand the nature of knowledge and then to elaborate what they see as the dimensions of truth within a particular area of knowledge. In the arguments presented by Young and his associates, questions of that kind are readily dismissed as ending with an absolutist view of knowledge. Young disposes superficially of absolutist frameworks and then embraces relativism and commitment as the only apparent alternatives. Yet there is within the sociology of knowledge a whole tradition of analysis which attempts to tread the path between absolute certainty and total relativism. Both sociologists and philosophers have asked significant questions in these areas which are, unfortunately, largely neglected in these most recent developments. Scheler, for example, takes what might be seen as a 'soft' view by arguing that only the selection of knowledge and relative levels of prestige are open to social influence. He makes it quite explicit that the content of the ideas themselves is not included in the analysis. Thus he writes that 'The sociological character of all knowledge, of all forms of thinking, perception, cognition is indubitable: not, of course, the content of all knowledge and still less its objective validity but the selection of its objects according to the ruling interest perspective.'[19]

Znaniecki similarly takes a 'soft' view, and warns against sociologists taking on epistemological questions. He argues that systems of knowledge,

> viewed in their objective composition, structure and validity – cannot be reduced to social facts, yet their historical existence within the empirical world of culture, in so far as it depends upon the men who construct them, maintain them by transmission and application, develop them or neglect them, must in large measure be explained sociologically. And this is what the sociology of knowledge has actually been doing whenever it was not vainly trying to become epistemology.[20]

Znaniecki is clear, therefore, that sociologists are not entitled to make judgements concerning the validity of systems of knowledge. Altogether it is possible to argue that the question of validation is central in any full discussion of knowledge and that the most recently developed arguments of the new sociologists of education pay insufficient regard to it. As Hamilton has noted, 'Validation in short is a difficult problem. It is tied up with the knowledge-differentiation processes, and, it must be recognised, cannot be adequately understood at a purely sociological level.[21]

It is being suggested, therefore, that a more discriminating approach to the sociology of knowledge would contain also a more explicit view of the nature of that area of study. This is a view, moreover, which would attempt to separate assertions about the nature of knowledge from observations about how people use knowledge.

None of this means abandoning the sociology of knowledge, unless that subject is seen as a means of undermining the bases of all knowledge. Instead it should enable the sociologist to concentrate on studies of the way in which knowledge is produced, distributed and legitimated. At the same time, it should encourage a concern for the ways in which such processes are interpenetrated by social phenomena. Thus it should be possible to develop a real sociology of the curriculum which would enable us to improve our understanding of the distribution of knowledge along with the relationship between the knowledge of subjects which teachers choose to employ and that which other practitioners of a subject might have. Such an approach would manifestly call for a significant sociology of examinations and assessment. In these ways we might come to an understanding of how, over time, subjects have been institutionalised in various types of schools, the processes by which, within subjects, certain knowledge is defined as 'important', and the consequences of those definitions for 'teacher' and 'taught'. The whole perspective would give a historical dimension to the sociology of education which it currently lacks. More importantly, however, it would help make explicit the issues arising from the differentiation of knowledge, whilst reducing the sociologist's attempt to tackle epistemological questions over diverse areas of knowledge.

An approach such as I am now recommending might usefully illuminate the ways in which, in educational institutions, ideologies have been made to serve a variety of functions. It may even encourage us to look anew at categories like 'progressive' and 'conservative' ideologies, as the earlier discussion on the development of the sociology of education in colleges has suggested. Moreover, such perspectives would not be irrelevant to the historically central interest of manpower requirements and social equality. As Bernstein has recently reminded us, most of the early work in the sociology of education focused upon 'the *demonstration*, not explanation of institutional sources of inequality in education'.[22] A sociology of the curriculum such as I have indicated could be an important beginning to developing explanations of inequality and educational failure. It would not need to treat the home or social class in a pathological fashion nor would it have as one of its main purposes the undermining of absolutism through all-out attacks on conventional criteria for educational success. An approach through knowledge and the curriculum could be the beginning of a relationship between understanding of 'classroom situations' and the ways in which these meanings are negotiated, as well as the 'structural' relationships which must be prior to the interactional elements. In these ways, movements in the content of education could be related to institutional arrangements which are external to the school. Similarly, as Bernstein has argued, following knowledge styles it might be important 'to consider range variation and change in what we can call organisational styles'.[23]

A comparative and historical concern with change and control in educational systems at both an institutional and a face-to-face level would develop readily from the proposals which have been outlined and would form a real basis for extending our knowledge of how the content of education has changed in relation to the changes brought about by industrialisation and changes in social stratification. At the same time it would be possible for sociologists to place emphasis upon the political decision-making process which determined the structure and content of education over time, and to the ideological framework in which those decisions were made.

If this were to be the field of the growing sociology of education, there still remains unresolved the problem of what might constitute the methods of enquiry and the nature of evidence in that field. There is a very real sense, however, in which this question cannot really be answered outside of a full discussion of the nature of the social sciences. A discussion of this kind is more suitably conducted in other places, but it is still possible to elaborate some of the relevant features particularly as much of this book has been concerned with the relationship between sociology and education.

Most especially, any revision of the sociology of education must look critically at the development of the subject over the last thirty years. As I have suggested throughout, one of the notable features of the sociology of education is its close association with, and interpenetration by, educational ideologies. One of the most distinctive elements of the educationalist context is the powerful influence of ideology and myth as against what might be simplistically termed 'science'. The straightforward attachment to science in human affairs is now readily and, to some degree, justly criticised by sociologists for offering too unproblematic a view of social science, and of societies. Nevertheless, aspects of its influence seem to have passed the educationalists by. A standpoint which leads to proposals that hypotheses might be verified only in operational terms has, over all, tended to enable its advocates to cut down the area of ideological dispute. As Birnbaum has said, such a standpoint has had 'in one sense, a liberating aspect : it was a sustained rejection of much that was inflated, irrelevant, and obscure in social discourse.'[24] It is precisely this sense of liberation and rejection that is missing from much educational debate, and towards which the new sociology of education seems unable to make any contribution.

Clearly one must not overestimate the achievement of science in the old sociology of education. There never was, for example, an articulated body of concepts, clearly verified hypotheses, approved by widely recognised and accepted techniques. Nor was it ever claimed that science could end the ideological debate by some kind of empirical decison. Indeed, as I have shown, amongst the most significant features of the old sociology of education was a strong dependence upon the educationalist context, a context which powerfully influenced both the teaching of the subject and the presentation of research findings. By its commitment, however, to certain modes of enquiry, the old sociology of education did, as Burns's analysis suggests, propose that it was possible to enlarge the scope of knowledge in human affairs. In this limited fashion, therefore, the best of the old sociology of education could undertake a dialogue with the advocates of educational ideologies. It might even be suggested that the most fruitful work of the early post-war development of the subject was the challenge offered to the prevailing traditionalist educational ideologies. The new sociology of education makes the distinction between itself and specific ideologies very unclear, and, as has been shown, this has important implications for truth and enquiry in the field of education.

The recent changes in educational practice and ideologies which emphasise cultural relativism in discussions of the school curriculum and the teacher's knowledge, and which represent attempts to equalise power between 'teacher' and 'taught', have been the context in which the new sociology of education has originated, and which, in turn, it has helped legitimise. It is for this reason that I have felt it important to discuss the genesis of both the old and the new sociologies of education and to describe the ways in which they have come to be accepted, whilst at the same time attempting to treat questions of truth and validity separately.

Both the old and new sociologies of education are not immune to ideological influence, but within the old there was contained the notion that it was possible to be wrong; that for any individual it will be impossible to describe reality independently of the conceptions we have available, but that, nevertheless, other concepts may turn out to be more useful and newer concepts may change our world view. It is this perspective which seem to be lacking in the more recent arguments.

Thus the inadequacies of the new sociology of education stem from its failure to face squarely the important theoretical, methodological and epistemological issues which are enmeshed in its development. The frequently obscure terms of much of its presentation serve to conceal that the discussions on relativism within the new sociology of education remain unsatisfactory. These discussions make little, if any, use of the long-standing philosophical debate on the topic, and never confront the difficulties which associate the more extreme forms of relativism with irrationalism. It is precisely to this question that Wilson's study of *Rationality* is devoted, yet it has hardly figured in the most recent debates. As Wilson points out, 'if comparison is to be made and if explanation is to occur by the relation of particular social processes and phenomena to more general propositions, at certain points the categories of the investigator must come into play'.[25] This, according to Lukes, might be called 'contextual rationality',[26] and, Wilson argues, once we have taken account of it, the empirical and rational procedures of science must be used if we are to understand these social processes. To understand a society, or a perspective within a society, in its own terms is not to explain it either anthropologically or sociologically, but to become completely assimilated socially. It is a pity that Wilson's warnings have not been heeded by at least some of the advocates of the new sociology of education. He shows us the difficulties of dismissing sociology as just another political perspective on the world, whilst at the same time he anticipates the most extreme penetration of the sociology of education by the new educational ideologies, a penetration which would assimilate teacher, taught and enquirer. It is this precisely to which Yardley draws our attention.

In a similar way it is to be regretted that the advocates of the new sociology of education have not taken up fully the arguments to be found in *Criticism and the Growth of Knowledge*.[27] Too frequently the advocates of the new sociology of education draw heavily upon many of the most recent changes in sociology. Yet they do so in a discrete and eclectic fashion, and fail to recognise the full significance of their claims. The issues they raise, however, are not merely of technical interest, but relate to the central concerns of knowledge and understanding. If explored they have implications not only for sociology and the sociology of education but also for the natural sciences. Lakatos recognises this and draws attention powerfully to the questions surrounding the standing of theories, empiricism and falsificationism.

As yet the new sociology of education is not represented by a large body of work, and consequently it is difficult to make an over-all assessment of what might be its 'findings'. It is easy to point to its ideological content and to its consequential uncertainties in the critical areas of the relationships between truth, knowledge and commitment. It would be easier to understand the significance of these uncertainties if they could be placed in a context which included, say, good sociological accounts of the development of knowledge in a particular topic and the ways in which that knowledge has been institutionalised in educational settings and is then 'handled' in classrooms.

In these matters, at least, the old sociology of education has certain advantages. It is open to public inspection and criticism, and whilst, as I have shown, it has been subjected to influence by the educationalist context in which it has developed and been taught, it has, nevertheless, struggled to maintain a dialogue with some of the educational ideologies. It has never totally conflated questions of truth and commitment, and it might even be that the tensions that have existed between the two have been the major means by which some educational hypocrisy and muddle have been cleared away. This does not seem inappropriate to a field like the sociology of education with its close connection with policy-making and political decision-taking. As the sociology of education develops, therefore, it is possible to hope that it might lead us to a more accurate description of educational arrangements and processes in a society. These arrangements and processes are real in the consequences which they have for members of a society, and it seems not unworthy to recognise this reality and to wish to come to a close understanding of it. Such an understanding may at all times be partial and, in an important sense, waiting for disproof, but it could nevertheless be distinguished from the hopes, commitments and ideologies of both sociologists and educationalists.

FURTHER READING

CENTRAL to the arguments developed in this study is a consideration of the work of Michael F. D. Young. It is important, therefore, that careful attention is given to his major work *Knowledge and Control: New Directions for the Sociology of Education* (London : Collier-Macmillan, 1971). This volume also contains G. Esland's influential article, 'Teaching and Learning as the Organisation of Knowledge', which is representative of the strong relativist position within the new sociology of education, a position which is elaborated by D. Gorbutt in 'The New Sociology of Education', *Education for Teaching* (Autumn 1972). The extension of Young's arguments can be found in the *Educational Review*, vol. 25 no. 3 (June 1973) ed. R. Meighan. This edition, entitled 'Sociology and Teaching', also contains some of the first attempts to provide a critical perspective on Young's work, and the article by M. D. Shipman, 'Bias in the Sociology of Education' is especially helpful. Suggestions of a modification in Young's position can be found in his article, 'Sociologists and the Politics of Comprehensive Education', *Forum* (Summer 1975).

Useful introductions to the diverse approaches of the sociology of knowledge can be found in J. E. Curtis and J. W. Petras, *The Sociology of Knowledge: A Reader* (London : Duckworth, 1970) Whilst Peter Hamilton's *Knowledge and Social Structure* (London : Routledge & Kegan Paul, 1974) presents some of the more recent developments in sociology in the context of the classical arguments in the sociology of knowledge. The historical development of the sociology of education can be followed through Jean Floud's and A. H. Halsey's trend report and bibliography in *Current Sociology*, vol. vii, no. 3 (1958). A helpful and tightly argued analysis of the growth of the subject in Britain can be found in Basil Bernstein's article, 'The Sociology of Education: a Brief Account', *Class, Codes, and Control* (London :

Routledge & Kegan Paul, 1972–3) vol. 3. In this article, Bernstein emphasises the ideological features of much of the contemporary debate within the sociology of education. Similarly, there are lively discussions of the relationship between sociology and education in *Sociology and Contemporary Education*, ed. Charles H. Page (New York : Random House, 1963).

Many of the philosophical and epistemological issues raised by Young and his associates are of the kind which are lucidly analysed by R. Trigg in his book *Reason and Commitment* (Cambridge University Press, 1972). Whilst for those who wish to examine further Popper's contribution to the debate about the nature of scientific enquiry can do so in *Conjectures and Refutations* or by way of introduction in B. Magee's *Popper* (London : Fontana, 1974) or P. Medawar's, *Induction and Intuition in Science* (London : Methuen, 1969). Developments and criticisms of Popper's views can be found in *Criticism and the Growth of Knowledge* (Cambridge University Press, 1970) ed. I. Lakatos and A. Musgrave, especially in the article by Lakatos. This book also contains useful criticism of the work of T. S. Kuhn and his major contribution *The Structure of Scientific Revolutions* 2nd edn (Chicago University Press, 1970).

REFERENCES

CHAPTER ONE

1.   M. F. D. Young (ed.), *Knowledge and Control: New Directions for the Sociology of Education* (London : Collier-Macmillan, 1971) p. 1.

2.   Ibid. p. 2.

3.   Ibid. p. 3.

4.   Ibid. p. 3.

5.   Ibid. p. 6; see also A. W. Gouldner, *The Coming Crisis of Western Sociology* (London : Heinemann, 1971).

6.   Ibid. p. 5.

7.   T. S. Kuhn, *The Copernican Revolution* (Harvard University Press, 1966), p. 265.

8.   R. Horton, 'Neo-Tylorianism; Sound Sense or Sinister Prejudice', *Man*, n.s., vol. 3 (1968).

9.   J. Douglas, *The Relevance of Sociology* (New York : Appleton-Century-Crofts, 1970).

10.   S. J. Eggleston (ed.), 'Editorial Introduction', *Contemporary Research in the Sociology of Education* (London : Methuen, 1974).

11.   B. Williamson, 'Continuities and Discontinuities in the Sociology of Education', in *Educability, Schools and Ideology*, ed. M. Flude and J. Ahier (London : Croom Helm, 1974) p. 3.

12.   K. Popper, 'The Sociology of Knowledge', in *The Sociology of Knowledge: A Reader*, ed. J. E. Curtis and J. W. Petras (London : Duckworth, 1970) p. 653.

13.   Young, *Knowledge and Control*, p. 24.

14.   Ibid. pp. 24–5.

15.   R. S. Peters, 'The Philosophy of Education', in *The Study of Education*, ed. J. W. Tibble (London : Routledge & Kegan Paul, 1966) p. 64.

16.   Ibid. p. 64.

17.   J. Floud and A. H. Halsey, 'The Sociology of Education', *Current Sociology*, vol. VII, no. 3 (1958).

18.   Ibid. p. 165.

19.   Ibid. p. 166.

20.   Ibid. p. 167.

21. Ibid. pp. 184, 193.
22. Ibid. p. 168.
23. Ibid. p. 169.
24. J. Floud, 'Social Class Factors in Educational Achievement', in *Ability and Educational Opportunity*, ed. A. H. Halsey (Organization for Economic Co-operation and Development, 1961) pp. 108, 91.
25. P. de Wolf and K. Härnqvist, quoted in *Equal Opportunity in Education* ed. H. Silver (London : Methuen, 1973) p. xxviii.
26. 1956 *White Paper on Technical Education*, in *Educational Documents England and Wales 1816–1963*, ed. J. S. Maclure (London : Chapman & Hall, 1965) p. 239.
27. 1959 *Crowther Report*, in ibid. p. 247.
28. Ibid. p. 249.
29. 1963 *The Robbins Report*, in ibid. pp. 297–8.
30. J. Vaizey, *Education for Tomorrow*, rev. edn (Harmondsworth : Penguin, 1966).
31. D. A. Goslin, *The School of Contemporary Society* (Illinois : Scott, Foresman, 1965) p. 45.
32. *Case Studies of Educational Innovation III – At the School Level* (Paris : O.E.C.D., 1973) p. 45.
33. J. Floud and A. H. Halsey, 'Introduction', in *Education, Economy and Society*, ed. A. H. Halsey, J. Floud and C. Arnold Anderson (New York : Free Press, 1963) p. 4.
34. Gouldner, *The Coming Crisis of Western Sociology*.

CHAPTER TWO

1. T. Burns, 'Sociological Explanation', *British Journal of Sociology*, vol. 18 (1967) p. 357.
2. Ibid. p. 358.
3. Quoted in M. Kogan (ed.), *The Politics of Education* (Harmondsworth : Penguin, 1971) pp. 91–2.
4. G. H. Bantock, *Education and Values* (London : Faber & Faber, 1965).
5. Quoted in Bantock, ibid. pp. 143, 141.
6. O. R. Brim, *Sociology and the Field of Education* (New York : Russell Sage Foundation, 1958) p. 75.
7. W. Taylor, 'The Sociology of Education in the Training College', *Education for Teaching* (Feb 1961) p. 46.
8. J. M. MacGuire, 'Sociology for Teachers', *Education for Teaching* (May 1963).
9. M. Shipman *et al.*, 'Association of Teachers in Colleges and

Departments of Education, Sociology Section', *Sociology in the Education of Teachers* (1969).

10. Ibid. p. 15.

11. See *Teaching Educational Psychology in Training Colleges* (London : British Psychological Society, 1962).

12. W. Taylor, *Society and the Education of Teachers* (London : Faber & Faber, 1969) p. 277.

13. Ibid. p. 279.

14. Ibid. p. 279.

15. A. Etzioni, in a review of E. Silberman, *Crisis in the Classroom* (New York : Random House, 1970). See *Harvard Educational Review*, 41 (1 Feb 1971) p. 93.

16. M. Bressler, 'The Conventional Wisdom of Education and Sociology', in *Sociology and Contemporary Education,* ed. C. H. Page (New York : Random House, 1963).

17. D. A. Hansen, 'The Uncomfortable Relation of Sociology and Education', in *On Education – Sociological Perspectives*, ed. D. A. Hansen and J. E. Gerstl (New York : Wiley, 1967).

18. Bressler, 'The Conventional Wisdom of Sociology and Education', p. 83.

19. *Teachers and Youth Leaders*, McNair Report (London : H.M.S.O., 1944) p. 71.

20. *The Government of Colleges of Education,* Weaver Report (London : H.M.S.O., 1966) p. 17.

21. Hansen, 'The Uncomfortable Relation of Sociology and Education', p. 14.

22. Bressler, 'The Conventional Wisdom of Sociology and Education', p. 91.

23. Gouldner, *The Coming Crisis of Western Sociology*, p. 343.

24. H. L. Elvin, *Education and Contemporary Society* (London : Watts, 1965) p. 34.

25. Quoted in G. Bernbaum, 'Sociology of Education', in *Education and its Disciplines,* ed. R. G. Woods (University of London Press, 1972) pp. 107–8.

26. For an exposition of Bernstein's views, see B. Bernstein, *Class, Codes and Control* (London : Routledge & Kegan Paul, 1972–3), vol. 1, 'Theoretical Studies towards a Sociology of Language', vol. 2, 'Applied Studies towards a Sociology of Language', vol. 3, 'Towards a Theory of Educational Transmissions'.

27. See H. Rosen, *Language and Class: a Critical Look at the Theories of Basil Bernstein* (Bristol : Falling Wall Press, 1972).

CHAPTER THREE

1. A. Giddens, *The Class Structure of the Advanced Societies* (London : Hutchinson, 1973) pp. 263–4.
2. R. Collins, 'Functional and Conflict Theories of Educational Stratification', in *Education: Structure and Society*, ed. B. R. Cosin (Harmondsworth : Penguin, 1972) p. 193.
3. I. Berg, *Education and Jobs – The Great Training Robbery* (Harmondsworth : Penguin, 1973).
4. J. Ford, *Social Class and the Comprehensive School* (London : Routledge & Kegan Paul, 1969).
5. J. C. Barker-Lunn, *Streaming in the Primary School* (Slough: National Foundation for Educational Research, 1970).
6. C. Jencks, 'Inequality in Retrospect', *Harvard Educational Review*, vol. 43, no. 1 (Feb 1973) p. 138.
7. C. Jencks, et al., *Inequality: A Reassessment of the Effect of Family and Schooling in America* (London : Allen Lane, 1974) p. 8.
8. S. I. Miller, 'Alternative School Systems : Jencks Reamined', *Intellect*, vol. 101, no. 2344 (Nov 1972) pp. 102–4.
9. A. R. Jensen, *Educational Differences* (London : Methuen, 1973).
10. H. J. Eysenck, *Race, Intelligence and Education* (London : Temple Smith in association with *New Society*, 1971).
11. R. J. Herrnstein, *I.Q. in the Meritocracy* (London : Allen Lane, 1973).
12. Giddens, *The Class Structure of the Advanced Societies.*
13. D. Holly, *Beyond Curriculum: Changing Secondary Education* (London : Hart-Davis, MacGibbon, 1973).
14. N. Keddie, *Tinker, Tailor . . . . The Myth of Cultural Deprivation* (Harmondsworth : Penguin, 1973).
15. C. and H. Rosen, *The Language of Primary School Children*, Schools Council Project on Language and Development in the Primary School (Harmondsworth : Penguin, 1973).
16. M. F. D. Young, 'Taking Sides Against the Probable Problems of Relativism and Commitment in Teaching and the Sociology of Knowledge', in 'Sociology and Teaching', ed. R. Meighan, *Educational Review*, vol. 25, no. 3 (June 1973) p. 210.
17. J. O'Neill, *Sociology as a Skin Trade* (London : Heinemann, 1972).
18. Young, 'Taking Sides Against the Probable', p. 213.
19. Ibid. p. 213.
20. Ibid. p. 216.
21. Ibid. p. 217.

22. Maurice Merleau-Ponty, *Humanism and Terror* (New York: Beacon Books, 1969).

23. Young, 'Taking Sides Against the Probable', p. 218.

24. Ibid. p. 218.

25. Ibid. p. 219.

26. Ibid. p. 221.

27. M. F. D. Young, 'Educational Theorizing: a Radical Alternative', *Education for Teaching* (Summer 1973) p. 11.

CHAPTER FOUR

1. O. Banks, 'The "New" Sociology of Education', *Forum, For the Discussion of New Trends in Education*, vol. 17, no. 1 (Autumn 1974) p. 6.

2. Williamson, 'Continuities and Discontinuities in the Sociology of Education'.

3. M. F. D. Young, 'Sociologists and The Politics of Comprehensive Education', *Forum, For the Discussion of New Trends in Education*, vol. 17, no. 3 (Summer 1975).

4. C. Searle, *This New Season* (London: Calder & Boyar, 1973) pp. 15, 8.

5. Ibid. p. 136.

6. H. Rosen, 'Message and Message Makers', *English in Education*, vol. 5, no. 2 (Summer 1971) p. 96.

7. E. P. Clark, 'Language and Politics in Education', *English in Education*, vol. 5, no. 2 (Summer 1971) p. 104.

8. C. Yardley, 'A Teacher's View', *Forum: For the Discussion of New Trends in Education*, vol. 17, no. 3 (Summer 1975) p. 101.

9. Ibid. p. 101.

10. G. Whitty, 'Sociology and the Problem of Radical Educational Change', in *Educability, Schools and Ideology*, ed. M. Flude and J. Ahier (London: Croom Helm, 1974) pp. 119, 116.

11. C. and H. Rosen, *The Language of Primary School Children*, pp. 15–16.

12. M. D. Shipman, 'Bias in the Sociology of Education', in 'Sociology and Teaching', ed. R. Meighan, *Educational Review*, vol. 25, no. 3 (June 1973).

13. D. A. Gorbutt, 'The New Sociology of Education', *Education for Teaching* (Nov 1972).

14. Whitty, 'Sociology and the Problem of Radical Educational Change'.

15. Eggleston, 'Editorial Introduction'.

16. Williamson, 'Continuities and Discontinuities in the Sociology of Education'.

17. Young, 'Sociologists and the Politics of Comprehensive Education'.

18. Bernstein, *Class, Codes and Control*, vol. 3, 'Towards a Theory of Educational Transmissions', pp. 156–7.

19. M. Scheler, 'The Sociology of Knowledge: Formal Problems', in *The Sociology of Knowledge – A Reader*, ed. J. E. Curtis and J. W. Petras (London : Duckworth, 1970) p. 175.

20. F. Znaniecki, 'Sociology and Theory of Knowledge', in ibid. p. 312.

21. P. Hamilton, *Knowledge and Social Structure* (London : Routledge & Kegan Paul, 1974) p. 150.

22. Bernstein, *Class, Codes and Control*, p. 149.

23. Ibid, p. 159.

24. N. Birnbaum, 'The Sociological Study of Ideology (1940–60): a Trend Report and Bibliography', *Current Sociology*, vol. ix, no. 2 (1960) p. 97.

25. B. Wilson (ed.), *Rationality* (Oxford : Blackwell, 1970) p. xvii.

26. In ibid.

27. I. Lakatos and A. Musgrave (eds), *Criticism and the Growth of Knowledge* (Cambridge University Press, 1970).